Bridging The Divide
Between Immigrant and
African-American Muslims
by Utilizing the Concept of
Tawheed as the Catalyst

Bridging The Divide Between Immigrant and African-American Muslims by Utilizing the Concept of Tawheed as the Catalyst

Imam Dr. Salahuddin Mustafa Muhammad

To order additional copies of this book, contact:
Xlibris Corporation
1-888-795-4274
www.Xlibris.com
Orders@Xlibris.com
96591

CONTENTS

ACKNOWLEDGEMENTS

Many thanks to Yusuf Ahmad (who has been my administrative clerk for many years at Fishkill Correctional Facility) for his help in typing and retyping my manuscript, no matter how many times I gave it back to him for revisions. I wish him well, for after thirty-eight years in prison he has just been granted parole. Two other clerks really helped me a lot with some technical details, Danny Hiraldo and Louis Burgh. I pray that they too are released soon. Thanks go out to Imam Warith Deen Mohammed, my leader, teacher and guide, and then to a host of imams and religious leaders for helping me to ground myself in the religion of Islam. Special thanks go to Professors Sherman Jackson, Ihsan Bagby, Jameelah Karim, Lawrence Mamiya, and Jimmie Jones for all of the constructive and supportive comments they gave me in preparing this manuscript. I have to thank those believers who believed in me enough to support me financially when money dried up. Thanks to the Shura Committee at Masjid Al Ikhlas and the entire community for giving me the time to complete this project. My thanks go out to Imam Ahsan Waris (Associate Imam of Masjid Al Ikhlas) for holding things down in my absence. Special thanks go out to the young people who worked with me as a part of the group. Finally, I would like to thank my family for excusing me for the many hours I needed to be away from them to complete my work, and special thanks goes out to my wife who has been my strongest supporter and toughest critic. Thank you Fonda, for all of your corrections and good advice. You are my rock. Any errors I have made or incorrect information I have conveyed are solely my responsibility, my spirit has always been Wa Allahu Alam! (And Allah Knows Best)!

ABOUT THE AUTHOR

Salahuddin Mustafa Muhammad a student of Islam since 1964 has developed into a very profound Islamic leader and propagator of the Islamic Religion within the Mid-Hudson Valley region and throughout New York State.

Imam Muhammad has received his Doctoral degree in Islamic Studies—Christian/Muslim relations from Hartford Seminary, a Masters degree in Theology and Counseling from New York Theological Seminary, and a Bachelor's degree in the Social Sciences from SUNY at New Paltz. He has also received a Graduate Certificate in Islamic Chaplaincy from Hartford Seminary. Imam Muhammad has a Certificate in Clinical Pastoral Education, and has completed hundreds of hours in Islamic studies and training from the Islamic Teaching Center in Indiana, where he has received certification in Imam training, the science of Qur'an, and **many other Islamic sciences**. He has also been a student of the late contemporary Islamic leader Imam Warith Deen Mohammed.

Imam Muhammad has been employed as a Muslim Chaplain for the New York State Department of Correctional Services since 1985, working in maximum, medium and minimum security prisons, county jails, as well as a psychiatric center. As a Muslim Chaplain, Imam Muhammad has propagated Islam with such intensity, and clarity that Allah has blessed many people to embrace Islam.

In 1986, Imam Muhammad became the resident Imam of **Masjid Al Ikhlas**, (formally Masjid Al Jihad Al Akbar), presently located in the City of Newburgh, where he is known for his 'DO IT NOW' attitude and zeal for establishing Islam. As a Muslim leader, he is known for his active and hands-on role in battling drugs, crime, gang violence, and prostitution within Orange County and the Mid-Hudson Valley region. Imam Muhammad is a member of numerous affiliations which include: **The Mosque Cares**, the National Association of Muslim chaplains, The North East Regional Majlis, The Greater Newburgh Ministerial Association, Dutchess County Clergy Association, the Islamic Society of North America and Muslim Alliance of North America. Imam Muhammad is the Amir (Leader) of the Mid-Hudson Valley Majlis. He is the first Muslim Chaplain hired by a college in the United States of America (Bard College 1996); and he has worked as an adjunct professor for Mercy and Marist colleges. He is also on the lecture circuit teaching and explaining the religion of Islam. Imam Muhammad believes in inter-faith dialogue and cooperation, he is a bridge builder who is constantly breaking down barriers that exist between Jews, Christians, and Muslims. He believes we all should be able to live together in peace.

Imam Muhammad is the recipient of the 2010 Human Rights Award from the Orange County Human Rights Commission. He has also received the Imam Umar Abdul Jalil Award for Spiritual Leadership from Citizens against Recidivism, October 30, 2009. He has received Proclamations and Certificates from the New York State Senate, Mayor of the City of Newburgh, Congressman and the County Executive of Orange County, New York. These Awards were for Exemplary Service as Imam and Leader in the community.

Imam Muhammad is the President of Newburgh Community Action Committee, and is an active Board member of Fortune Society in New York City. He has made the Hajj to the Holy City of Mecca in 1990 and then again in the year 2000. Imam Muhammad has published an article called, "Healers From Within-The Role of Muslim Prison Chaplains." He also published an article titled' "Neighbors: From a Muslim Perspective."

Finally, Imam Muhammad is a proud husband of his dedicated and supportive wife, Fonda, father of four beautiful sons, and a lovely daughter, and has seven lovely grandchildren.

As a firm believer, Imam, husband, father, and propagator of Islam, Imam Muhammad, has indeed grown to become an excellent example of how a Muslim should imitate Allah Ta'Ala's example for humanity, and that is Prophet Muhammad (Peace be upon him).

PREFACE

The Islamic community boasts of being one united community. Its cornerstone belief is *Tawheed* (oneness of G-d). Its fundamental principle is the Unity of G-d, and this speaks to the unity of humanity. Yet when you look at the Islamic community over its almost fifteen century history, racism, prejudice, bias, and discrimination have continued to prevail.

I argue that the Islamic community has suffered fragmentation, as a result of this artificial divide. Therefore, the one united community has been more of an ideal than reality.

I contend that really understanding the concept of *Tawheed* is the true answer—the bridge—as it were—to overcoming this artificial divide, the divide that separates the immigrant Muslim from the African American Muslim.

Because immigrants have come to America with a lot of cultural baggage, pre-conditioned notions, biases, prejudices, etc., I decided to work with young people who had less baggage. Between January 2009 and July 2009, I held weekly classes with six young men and six young women from various ethnic and cultural backgrounds. Their ages ranged from thirteen to seventeen. I utilized Cognitive Restructuring as my theoretical construct. The idea being if you can change the way a person thinks, you can change their behavior. I taught classes on the three aspects of *Tawheed* and conveyed its practical importance that should be translated in our everyday lives. I also taught the meaning of *Aqeedah,* which is the most important belief from which *Tawheed* originated. I conducted Socratic Seminars, showed DVDs, and had students perform skits, as well as role play. The students had to give oral presentations and write a journal. Emphasis was put on the Hajj (pilgrimage to the Holy City of Mecca) as the ideal situation demonstrating the oneness of the community.

Imam Dr. Salahuddin Mustafa Muhammad

FOREWORD

Imam Salahuddin Muhammad has made a significant contribution to the literature in his study, "Bridging the Divide Between Immigrant and African American Muslims by Utilizing the Concept of Tawheed as the Catalyst." Research studies have always shown that Muslim masajid (mosques) in the United States have among the highest rates of interracial worship in their Friday Jumu'ah services. More than 90% of the mosques reported that there were more than one ethnic or racial group attending the services. This phenomenon stands in contrast to Christian churches where only 7% of the churches have multi-ethnic congregations on Sunday mornings and 93% remain dominated by one racial group. As Dr. Martin Luther King, Jr. once remarked, "Sunday mornings at 11 a.m. remain the most segregated hour in American society." While Muslim mosques have a fine record of interracial worship, research studies have also shown that there is still a great deal of tension between immigrant and African American Muslims. Outside of the worship service, they seldom socialize together and they continue to hold stereotypes about each other.

In his quest to overcome the racial tensions and stereotypes and to uphold the Muslim ideal of a universal Ummah (community), Imam Muhammad has used his own multiethnic mosque, Masjid Al-Ikhlas in Newburgh, to test the possibility of using the concept of Tawheed (the oneness and unity of Allah) as the catalyst to bridge the divide between immigrant and African American Muslims. Since older Muslims tend to bring a lot of cultural and ethnic baggage with them, Imam Muhammad decided to work with the young people at the mosque, holding weekly classes with six young men and six young women from different ethnic and cultural backgrounds. These classes focused on the various aspects of Tawheed in everyday life, using seminars, DVDs, skits and role-playing. The students gave oral presentations and kept a weekly journal. He also placed emphasis on the Hajj (pilgrimage to Mecca) as the ideal situation, which demonstrates the oneness of the community. As El-Hajj Malik El-Shabazz (Malcolm X) testified in his autobiography, the Hajj became the turning point in his life when he saw all of the diverse races and classes of humankind gathered together as one community in performing the rituals of the Hajj. It is this practical achievement of the ideal of oneness of Allah and the oneness of community that Imam Muhammad desires to demonstrate in the everyday life of Muslims in his masjid.

Lawrence H. Mamiya, Ph.D.
Professor of Religion and Africana Studies
Vassar College

To three that I hold dear to my heart, my mother who passed three days after her 79th birthday in 2009. She was always there for me. She always believed in me and always gave of herself selflessly. To Imam Warith Deen Mohammed (who passed on September 9th 2008), my instructive guide who taught me how to be the leader and true human being that I am. And to my beloved wife Fonda who has been a great source of inspiration to me and has constantly and consistently been my support. These three by Allah's leave made me who I am. For this I am forever grateful.

"The greatest discovery in our generation is that human beings,
by changing the inner attitude of their minds,
can change the outer aspects of their lives."-William James
(The varieties of Religious Experience)

INTRODUCTION

For better than fourteen centuries Muslims have boasted of being one united community under the banner of *La Ilaha Ill Allah, Muhammadur Rasulillah.*[1] Muslims have espoused this doctrine of *Tawheed* (oneness) stating emphatically that Muslims are one and not divided. However, if you take a closer look at the history of Muslims throughout the world, you see a very different picture.

What you see is that although Muslims speak about the unity and oneness of the *ummah* (community), the community is divided along racial, cultural, tribal, ethnic, national, and class lines. This reality calls into question the notion of unity among Muslims ever being something truly realized. Have Muslims ever realized this ideal, or has it been illusory, a utopia if you will, not yet fully realized?

I believe that it is achievable, although it calls for Muslims to truly grasp the concept of *Tawheed* and really put it into action. I believe that the Muslim world has suffered from divisiveness because the pristine message of *Tawheed* has escaped the many. It is one thing to be able to expound on *Tawheed* and its various aspects, but to apply it is yet another.

I intend to delve into the concept of *Tawheed,* to show what it truly means and how it is to be applied in the Muslim's life. A colleague once told me that "you don't have to try to boil the ocean." It was a timely conversation because the project seemed too huge. I decided that I would concentrate on working with a group of young people at our Masjid.

The idea of working with young people appealed to me because I believed this group would be more receptive to venturing out from their cultural habitats. Older people are more set in their ways. If they have been brought up a certain way, the likelihood of them changing is not that good. Change takes a lot of concerted effort. It takes a lot of work that, in my opinion, the average person is not willing to do.

The group consisted of twelve students, six boys and six girls. The ages of these students ranged from thirteen to seventeen. The ethnic breakdown was Pakistani, Puerto Rican, Bangladeshi, African, African-American, Moroccan, and Trinidadian.

---

[1]   In English this means there is none worthy of worship, except Allah, and Muhammad is the Messenger of Allah. When we say Prophet Muhammad's name it is customary to say, "May the Peace and blessings of Allah be upon Him.

The project initially started as a four-month program but went for an additional two months.

The group met every Sunday from 11:00 a.m. to 12:30 p.m. The class sessions were expanded on some occasions because of the topics discussed, workshops, or Socratic Seminars conducted.[2] The six months were filled with power point presentations, skits, and other role-playing activities. The students made presentations affirming the beauty of their culture. We will show that these affirmations demonstrated that in diversity there is unity and that this is what G-d[3] wants for us.

I conducted a semi-structured interview with the students to see what they thought about race, ethnicity, culture, class, etc. The outcome of these interviews showed that the students were impacted by their cultural upbringing to an extent, but they were more impacted by the society in which they live.

Because young people learn differently, we made sure that we utilized the different styles of teaching to insure that we reached everyone. We utilized the concept of Multiple Intelligences.[4] Recognizing that everyone does not learn the same, we made sure that we in some way utilized a methodology that touched on the verbal/linguistic, logical/mathematical, visual/spatial, bodily/kinesthetic, musical/rhythmic, interpersonal, intrapersonal, and naturalist ways to make sure that all the students got it. The classes were lively and exciting, and the students enjoyed being a part of the program.

Chapter one deals with the history of Masjid Al Ikhlas as an up and coming Islamic community. This chapter will give the reader important insight into the make up of the community and how we, after so many years of struggle, got to where we are today. It is in this chapter that we begin to identify some of the challenges that face our community.

In chapter two the roots of our challenge and the baggage we bring are discussed.

The historical and cultural roots of certain problems that have festered in the Muslim community for centuries are examined and discussed.

In chapter three the concept of *Tawheed* in its various manifestations, showing how important this concept is to the survival and thriving of the Islamic community.

---

[2]   *www.studyGuide.org/Socratic Seminar.htm* The Socratic method of teaching is based on Socrates' Theory that it is more important to enable students to think for themselves than to merely fill their heads with "Right" answers. Therefore, he regularly engaged his pupils in dialogues by responding to their questions with questions, instead of answers. This process encourages divergent thinking rather than convergent.

[3]   The writer chooses to use this way of writing G-d in respecting his leader's understanding and respect for calling the Creator by that name, as god spelled backwards spells dog.

[4]   David Lazear, *EIGHT WAYS OF TEACHING—The Artistry of Teaching with Multiple Intelligences,* SkyLight Professional Development, Arlington Heights, Il. 1991.

This chapter really lays out the cornerstone of what truly is Muslim life. It is in this chapter that *Tawheed* will clearly be seen as the ideal principle and foundation for establishing the community that the Prophet Muhammad espoused for twenty-three years.

In chapter four the components of Cognitive Restructuring, the theoretical construct utilized in the six-month program is examined. The central concept is, "Change the way the person thinks and you will be able to change the way the person acts (behaves)." The writer will show, using this model, that knowledge comes first and then the action follows. The writer acknowledges that there is another educational construct that favors actions preceding knowledge; nevertheless, it will be shown that evidence for knowledge preceding actions is what is more prevalent in today's society among learning professionals.

In chapter five the ministry project itself is discussed. In this chapter the reader will be taken through what was done with the students in the six-month project. The reader will be taken through the various phases of the project, and how the concept of *Tawheed* was introduced to the students and how they responded to the concept.

Chapter six is the concluding chapter. In this chapter, the six-month program is evaluated and our findings are presented. The program will be described and a summary of what seems to work, and what did not work, and what the future seems to hold will all be examined.

CHAPTER 1

THE ISLAMIC COMMUNITY
IN NEWBURGH

Masjid Al Ikhlas—the Mosque of Sincerity /Purity (formally known as Masjid Al Jihad Al Akbar) is the very first Masjid (Mosque) to be established in Orange County, New York. Masjid Al Ikhlas is located in the City of Newburgh, New York. Newburgh is 60 miles north of New York City, and 90 miles south of Albany, on the Hudson River. The population was 28,259 at the 2000 census. Figures released by the U.S. Census Bureau in late June 2009 estimated that the population at that time was 28,101.[5] In terms of demographics the racial makeup of the city was 42.33% White, 32.96% Black or African American, 0.07% Native American, 0.76% Asian, 0.06% Pacific Islander, 18.11% from other races, and 5.07% from two or more races. Hispanic or Latino of any race was 36.30% of the population.[6]

The history of the Masjid begins with its people. Before there was a physical edifice, some Muslims started meeting in Bloomingburg, New York (about eight miles north of Middletown, New York). The Muslims were meeting at the Imam's house. The Imam at that time was Imam Warith Deen Umar. There were about four or five families who would come together. In 1986 Imam Umar moved to Albany, because of a promotion and job change. He recommended the writer, Salahuddin M. Muhammad, to be the Imam of this small group and the group accepted his recommendation.

As the leadership of this community changed hands, a lot of new energy came to the community. The Muslim families began to meet at the new Imam's house in Middletown. Instead of meeting once a month on Sundays, we began to meet on Fridays for *Jumu'ah* services. The Islamic community continued to grow, and as a result of this growth, we had to find another place to meet that would be more accommodating. In our sojourn, we met in the City of Newburgh at the N.A.A.C.P.

---

[5]   *http://quickfacts.census.gov/qfd/states/36/3650034.html*

[6]   Ibid.

building on Liberty Street for a little while, as the community continued to grow. Because of this growth the community could no longer meet at the N.A.A.C.P. building, and we subsequently began to meet in Downing Park.

The Islamic community continued to search for a suitable place and finally moved into a storefront in the quaint City of Beacon, New York, across the Hudson River. It was a glorified storefront that we intended to use only temporarily, because our vision was set upon being established in our own Masjid somewhere in Orange County, New York. There were already three Masajid (Mosques) in Dutchess County. One Mosque was right in Beacon. (Some of the Members of our Masjid decided that they should be in leadership, and therefore set up their own Masjid). There is a Masjid in Wappingers Falls, New York (which happened to be the first Masjid built from the ground up), and there is a building in the City of Poughkeepsie that was turned into a Masjid.

In 1987, the Islamic community under this writer's leadership became incorporated as a 501 C (3) Non-For-Profit religious organization. In the same year, the Islamic community received its tax-exempt status. Along with the articles of incorporation, we have by-laws (see appendix A), which give our community organization and structure. The by-laws spell out the formalities of how the community is run.[7] Those who become a part of the community are given a copy of the by-laws to give them a good picture of how we govern ourselves. It actually lets them know how we function. Carl S. Dudley calls this "The formal process which includes practices, procedures, and policies that have been openly considered and officially accepted by the congregation."[8] Everyone who comes through the door and wants to know how we formally function as a community needs to read the by-laws. Article VI states, "Overriding authority is had first by the Noble Qur'an and then by the authentic Sunnah of the Prophet Muhammad.

The community continued to grow and continued to have various types of fundraisers to raise money for the establishment of a Masjid in Orange County. The breakthrough came in 1992. The treasurer at the time, Melody Rashada, and her husband Hamin Rashada (my assistant), spotted the building we are presently in. The building was an old warehouse situated on 9/10ths of an acre, right in the middle the City of Newburgh. The building cost $175,000. We purchased the building by negotiating an interest free mortgage. Needless to say, spirits were very high.

---

7   Masjid Al Ikhlas By-Laws developed and ratified in 1990. The last amendment made to it was on Sunday January 13th 2008. These By-Laws are used to govern the community.

8   Carl S. Dudley, *Studying Congregations, A New Handbook*, Abingdon Press, Nashville, TN, 1998, 107.

We turned that old warehouse into a dignified house of worship, a Masjid. We had a balloon payment of $135,000 to pay in two years. Looking back over the situation years later, it shows that we were pretty naïve to think that we could raise that amount of money. Although it was a big amount, our faith and high hopes were much bigger. We therefore continued to do fundraising activities, selling dinners, bulk mail—outs, advertising, and trying to get financial support from Saudi Arabia and any other Islamic country of which we were aware. Name it and we did it to try and raise the money needed.

We only raised $35,000 toward the balance of the mortgage payment that was due in 1994. We decided to go back to the sellers to renegotiate the payments, and by the leave of G-d, the sellers accepted our new proposal. We were blessed to receive additional financial help from some of the immigrant Muslims in the community. To make a long story short, these gracious brothers came up with $40,000, which gave us a total of $75,000 cash. We gave the sellers that amount and worked out a monthly installment plan to take care of the balance. In the meantime, we continued to raise money through fundraising and were able to pay off the previous owners in 1998.

Since we were the only Masjid in Orange County at the time, immigrant Muslims began to join our ranks. The community went from five families to thirty-five families, to seventy-five families, to one hundred families (see appendix B historical timeline).

The complexion of the community changed from being one particular ethnic group (African American) to being many ethnic groups. The African American Muslims who started the Islamic work in the area were now in the minority. With so many Muslims coming out to the Friday prayer service, it became evident that the place was really too small to accommodate the growing Muslim community.

After thirteen years of being part of the Newburgh community, we started the second phase (which was to build from the ground up). Actually, before this we made renovations about three times. We expanded our Masjid by building a new prayer hall right alongside the first structure. The Masjid construction was completed in 2007. The complete job cost $500,000. The new edifice has a domed minaret and looks like an authentic Middle Eastern Mosque. One of the local newspapers asked one of the Rabbis what he thought about the new constructed Masjid and he said, "It was the Taj Mahal of Newburgh." Masjid Al Ikhlas became a Masjid (as one news reporter mentioned when he was doing an article on us) where you can find people from almost every part of the world.

The Masjid is presently full of Pakistanis, Bangladeshis, Indians, Arabs, Africans, Latinos, Caucasians, and African Americans. In looking at the Masjid as a congregation, it is apparent that the Islamic community is ultimately governed by the just dictates of the Qur'an (The Word of G-d) and the Sunnah (Words and

Actions of His Prophet and Messenger Muhammad); however, it still has to operate within a particular context.[9]

As mentioned earlier, Masjid Al Ikhlas has in place organizational rules, policies, and procedures. It has articles of incorporation and by-laws that are set up to give it structure. The Masjid has a board of trustees that oversees the entire operation of the Masjid. It has a system in place that offers checks and balances. The Masjid utilizes the corporate as well as the religious structure. The leader of the Masjid is the Imam (prayer leader), although within this society, the role of the Imam is seen as the leader in every respect. In our Masjid the key players are the Imam, the treasurer, the secretary, and the board of trustees, which is called the *Shura* (consultation) committee. The *Shura* committee is the decision making group that meets monthly to discuss Masjid business. They are responsible for the smooth operation of the Masjid. It was not always set up this way, however, by structuring it this way the community is not run by just one individual. A collective body oversees the Masjid's operation.

The board of trustees is set up to reflect the diversity that is present in our Islamic community. In fact, unlike most boards set up in various Islamic communities around the country, out of seven board members, three are female. This shows that the Masjid truly values the insight and knowledge that women bring to the meetings. The understanding is if women represent fifty percent of the community, not involving them in leadership would be to deny ourselves an integral partner in the growth and development of our community.

Presently, on the *Shura* committee we have three African American women, one African American man, one Indian man, one Pakistani man, and one Bangladeshi man. All of them happen to be professional people. Three are chaplains for the Department of Corrections; two are medical doctors, one is a businessman, and one is a schoolteacher. The community votes these board members in. These board members are able to establish policy for our community.[10]

As the Imam of the community, I am the religious leader and, therefore, act as an advisor to the board, although I do not have a vote on the board. In reality, I do not need a vote because, as the Imam, I have a great deal of influence in the community.

---

[9] Lee G. Bolman and Terrence E Deal, *Reframing Organizations*, Jossey-Bass, San Francisco, CA 2003, 14.

[10] Masjid Al Ikhlas By-Laws developed and ratified in 1990. The last amendment made to it was on Sunday January 13th 2008. These By-Laws are used to govern the community.

The Islamic community is a community that values community life.[11] Community life is very important to Muslims. Muslims are told that they are to love for their brother what they love for themselves.[12] Muslims are further told that they are like one human body: if one part hurts the whole body hurts.[13] Muslims come together under the banner of "There is none that deserves to be worshipped except G-d and Muhammad is His slave-servant and Messenger." Although this unites Muslims, one still witnesses particular feelings, attitudes, and prejudices from some of the community members. All of these feelings, attitudes, and prejudices need to be worked on because they can cause a community to be divided. Many of these characteristics are the individual's cultural baggage. It becomes the leader's responsibility to guide the community away from such hurtful and destructive characteristics that are not a part of the Islamic teachings or practices. On the contrary, Islam teaches against such attitudes, feelings, and behaviors.

Masjid Al Ikhlas has various ethnic groups that have come together to form one united community, albeit superficially. This ethnically diverse community is seen as an asset, because it speaks to the universality of the religion. Because the community is so ethnically rich, we have to develop programs that will satisfy everyone. There is a conscientious effort on my part not to offend anyone. Regardless of the different feelings, attitudes, and prejudices the Muslims bring with them to the community, I work hard to present Islam in a way that the believers can appreciate. My having (by G-d's grace) a good, solid understanding of the religion helps the situation. I do not favor any particular school of thought, but take from all of them what I believe is closest to the Qur'an and the Sunnah.

It does not matter what country one comes from; there are some very fundamental beliefs that we all share as Muslims. When we articulate those fundamental beliefs in the right way, the community of Muslims rally around the leader with undying support. When one treats the members of the community with the highest degree of respect, they endear themselves to the person. I also think it is equally important to get the community members involved in masjid activities.

The Islamic community is molded and shaped by its two sacred texts, which for Muslims are the Noble Qur'an and the authentic Sunnah. Muslims believe the

---

[11] Lee G. Bolman And Terrence E. Deal, *Reframing Organizations*, (Jossey-Bass, San Francisco, CA 2003), 14.

[12] 100 Ahadith about manners, compiled by Research Division, Darussalam, Riyadh, Saudi Arabia 200, 14.

[13] Al Imam Abu Zakariya bin Sharaf an-Nawawi ad-Dimashqi, Riyadh-Us-Saliheen, vol. 1, Published by Darussalam Publishers & Distributors, Riyadh, 1998, 228.

Noble Qur'an to be "the Word of G-d in exact word and meaning"[14] The Sunnah (way) of the Prophet Muhammad is a detailed map of what should be understood and followed.[15] Muslims believe that the Noble Qur'an and the authentic Sunnah together represent a divine package. This package is called the *Sharia* (Islamic Law). The root for the word *Sharia* means path to water. The meaning is that this is the path to the source of all life. Muslims drink from this water to sustain their lives.[16] Interestingly, Robert Schreiter speaks about mapping a local theology by recognizing the "dynamic interaction," among the Qur'an and Sunnah, Mosque and Culture.[17] Everything in the community revolves around the Noble Qur'an and the authentic Sunnah. The Muslim identity is shaped and sustained by it. From the Muslim perspective, a person's culture is not altered as long as it complies with what Islam represents. If the culture does not comply, then it is to be rejected. The foundation of a Muslim's life is the Qur'an and Sunnah. This is what influences them and helps to develop their Muslim identity. One may then ask, "What is the role of the Imam in all of this?"

The Imam's role is like that of a mother. Imam actually comes from the Arabic root *Alif Meem*. These two letters are the same letters for *umm*, which is the Arabic word for mother.

The Imam, like a mother, provides for the community's spiritual nourishment. He nurtures, molds, shapes, and helps to develop what is in the womb (environment). He has the awesome responsibility of inspiring the Islamic community with the Word of G-d and His Messenger. This speaks to the Imam's capacity to develop the life of the congregation, which is a womb of development and growth. He stands on the *Mimbar* (similar to a podium) and infuses the spirit of the believers. Every Friday, the Imam gives a relevant talk to the congregants to keep the Word of G-d always in front of them. The main idea communicated to the Muslims is that G-d is one alone without partners, and that Muhammad, the son of Abdullah, is His slave-servant and Messenger. This idea of oneness is called *Tawheed*.

The Islamic community develops a sense of oneness in that the community keeps close to this powerful motif. Although all Muslims accept the *Kalima Shahada* (the statement that I bear witness that none deserves to be worshiped except Allah,

---

14 Ahmed Von Denffer, *Ulum-Al-Qur'an*, an introduction to the sciences of the Qur'an, Published by the Islamic foundation, United Kingdom, 1983, 17.

15 Jamaal Al-Din M. Zarobozo, *The Authority and Importance of the Sunnah*, Published by Al-Basheer Company for publications and translations, Denver, CO, 2000, 14-15.

16 Ahmad Hasan, *Principles of Islamic Jurisprudence, The command of the Shariah and Juridical Norm*, (Published by Islamic Research Institute, Islamabad, Pakistan), 1993, 1.

17 Robert J. Schreiter, *Constructing Local Theologies*, Published by Orbis Books, MaryKnoll, N.Y. 1985, 148.

and I bear witness that Muhammad is the servant and Messenger of Allah), many hold onto the theological beliefs that come from their cultures. This happens, of course, in a syncretistic way. For example, many African American Muslims (coming from a Christian background), have more of a Christian understanding of theology than a Muslim one.

There are even some Muslims from other countries that have a conception of G-d that is not exactly the Islamic concept. It is my duty to teach Islam in its pristine purity. I am in the habit of teaching what the correct belief is, always with the hope that the Muslims are grasping what I am teaching. Based on the feedback that I have been receiving, I am getting the point of correct belief *(Aqeedah)* out to the people. How we see G-d is very important. In our belief, G-d is not a spirit. G-d creates spirits. Muslims do not believe that a spark of the divine is in all of us as other faiths do.

Schreiter speaks about dual religious systems.[18] Some Muslim converts to Islam embrace the religion, but they also continue to practice other traditions. For example, there is not a belief in Astrology, yet some Muslims continue to believe in it and practice it. Some of these converts also participate in Kwanzaa celebrations during the Christmas holidays. Likewise, Muslims who come from overseas oftentimes bring with them cultural baggage. These cultural practices are not Islamic, but in their minds it is absolutely part of the faith.

An example of this is Muslims going to the graves of their dead relatives and praying to them to intercede on their behalf in this world as well as the next. This aspect is clearly an act of *Shirk* (setting up partners with G-d). Many Muslims in America, indigenous as well as immigrant, have adopted the American culture, e.g., listening to a lot of music, going to movies, watching television, frequenting amusement centers, having Western style weddings, baby showers, etc. I actually witnessed an Albanian Muslim family in the Newburgh Mall over the Christmas holidays allow their young son to sit on the lap of Santa Claus! This is clearly unIslamic, but it is done nevertheless with no thought of doing anything wrong.

The threat of disunity exists in our community due to various forces, e.g., racial, ethnic, national, and cultural considerations. These considerations cause individuals to think they are better than or superior to others (specifically better than or superior to African Americans) because of these superficial, albeit, artificial considerations. These various forces, generally speaking, cause immigrant Muslims to have a superiority complex and cause the African American Muslim to have an inferiority complex. This is not unlike what African Americans experienced from

---

[18]   Robert J. Schreiter, *Constructing Local Theologies*, Published by Orbis Books, Maryknoll, NY. 1985, 148.

the way Caucasian Americans have treated them in the past—from the plantation life until now. Paul Barrett recently wrote, "Black Muslims often get slighted by their co-religionist, sometimes out of plain racism."[19]

With the heavy influx of immigrants to the community, there have been growing tensions between different groups. I have heard African Americans complain that they feel like the immigrants treat them like second class Muslims. They do not feel like the immigrant Muslims accept them on an equal basis. I dare say that some of this may be the African American Muslim's paranoia or his or her own sense of inadequacy or insecurity. However, I believe there is some truth in what they say or believe. Dr. Joy Degruy Leary calls it Post Traumatic Slave Syndrome (PTSS). She traces the way that both overt and subtle forms of racism have damaged the collective African American psyche.[20]

The late Imam Warith Deen Mohammed addressed the residue of plantation life for over three decades. His ministry was instrumental in helping me personally, and many African Americans in general, to accept ourselves as being dignified and honorable, and as being as good as anyone else. African Americans who have suffered from being told they were 3/5ths of a man, to being chattel slaves, have longed to be treated equally by others. They truly believe that all people are created equal. Islam supports this belief and *Tawheed* is the foundation of it. Therefore, for African Americans, having a true understanding of *Tawheed* is truly liberating.

Since our community is mostly immigrant, some of the immigrant members would prefer to have an immigrant imam because this is what they are used to having.

It is also evident that there are some differences in styles of leadership practiced by immigrant Muslims and African American Muslims. We have recently hired an immigrant imam to lead the prayers and help with *Jumu'ah* (the Friday prayer service) though I am still the senior Imam of the community—an African American Imam leading a predominantly immigrant community.

Usually the immigrant Imam is just the prayer leader and has no real authority in the Masjid. On the other hand, the African American Imam is usually the authority of the Masjid. I have shared some of my authority over the years and invested it into the *Shura* committee (Board of Trustees) to insure that there is no demagoguery. This is quite extraordinary because traditionally the African American Imam is the authority in the Masjid. He has the final word. In the immigrant community the board of trustees has the final word, or the president of the center. What I have

---

[19]   Paul Barrett, *American Islam the Struggle for the soul of a religion*, (Farrar, Staus and Giroux), NYC, 2005, 129.

[20]   Dr. Joy Degruy Leary, *Post Traumatic Slave Syndrome: America's Legacy of Enduring Injury and Healing*, *Uptone* Press, Milwaukee, Oregon, 2005.

tried to do is to have the best of both worlds. I am the Imam, however, the *Shura* committee oversees the running of the Masjid.

For our Masjid, it does not seem unusual to have an African American senior Imam over a predominantly immigrant community. Today we have an African American President over the United States of America even though African Americans only represent 13% of the entire population. It should not matter. What should matter is that the best person is in the job. I have been the Imam from the beginning and just because the complexion of the community changes, the Imam does not have to be changed. My being the Imam makes quite a difference and sometimes causes a little stir because I am not beholden to anyone based on his or her race, ethnic, national, or cultural identity. I try my level best to be balanced, taking my lead from the Prophet Muhammad. We do all that we can to make our community a balanced community.

As the Imam of the community, I have to keep the Islamic community grounded in the religion, free from distortion and misrepresentation. It is my responsibility to teach the religion from the pure sources without pushing a particular school of thought, taking into consideration the many Muslims that are part of our community. I have to show that there is indeed unity in our diversity. I have to get them to truly understand the concept of *Tawheed*.

Even though I am the Imam, there are so many challenges. The challenges of disunity, disagreement, authority issues, cultural insensitivities, biases, prejudices, etc., come up from time to time. Trying to reason with some of the Muslims is to no avail. The older Muslims are so set in their ways that it seems almost an impossible task to change them. The reality is they are not interested in changing. They are fine just the way they are.

Therefore, I have decided rather than to continue butting heads, I will spend that quality time teaching their children. This seemed like the best thing to do because there would naturally be less resistance to change on the part of the children. This would be a great opportunity to foster the growth in the children that we want to see in the future of our community. The concentration would be laying out the proper Islamic foundation, which, in my opinion, would ground the children in the fundamental basics of the religion, free of any cultural or racial bias or prejudicial considerations.

There is an old expression that says, "Those who fail to learn from their past are doomed to repeat it." We therefore take on the challenge of delving into the historical and cultural roots of the problems infecting our community.

CHAPTER 2

THE ROOTS OF OUR CHALLENGE
AND THE BAGGAGE WE BRING

Masajid (Mosques) have been popping up all over the United States of America. These Mosques have been storefronts, renovated buildings, churches, synagogues, and some have been built from the ground up. These Mosques have been mostly ethnic. One could find a Mosque of African Americans, a Pakistani Mosque, an Arab Mosque, a Turkish Mosque, an Albanian Mosque, etc. For any ethnic group, one could find a Mosque completely dominated by that group. It seemed that every group sought to find comfort within their own ethnic or racial grouping.

But Imam Feisal Abdul Rauf gives a hint at the problem that comes as a result of this.

> Islam spread from the Arabian Peninsula to the rest of what is known today as the Muslim world. It had to restate its religious principles in the cultural context of ancient pre-Islamic societies: Egypt, Mesopotamia, Turkey, Iran, Africa, India and so forth. And we witness shades of differences between Egyptian Islam and Indian Islam, between Turkish Islam and Senegalese Islam—not in theology but in sociology and laws that flowed from different pre-existing customs of each society.[21]

As previously mentioned, it is these customs and cultures that have caused so much division in the Muslim community. Imam Rauf mentions Africa and then mentions Senegalese Islam. What about the other countries in Africa? Each of them has its own customs and cultures.

The same is true with India or Pakistan or Bangladesh for that matter. It is what I call the Muslim Identity that we as Muslims should take on; Imam Rauf calls it the

---

[21]   Imam Feisal Abdul Rauf, *What's right with Islam, A New Vision for Muslims in the West* (New York: Harper Collins 2005), 258.

American Islamic Identity. We are basically saying the same thing. What is needed is a merger of immigrant Muslim identities with African American Muslim identities. This is especially needed here in America, as America has become the permanent home of immigrant Muslims today.

I was involved with a Mosque that was dominated by African Americans. The group was affiliated with the late Imam Warith Deen Mohammed, the son of Elijah Muhammad. After 9/11 many immigrants began to move to our area and our Masjid eventually over time evolved into a multi-ethnic, multi-cultural Masjid. Because of all these groups coming together, tensions began to rise. There were disputes and arguments. Some Muslims have said to me, as I sat with them trying to resolve a dispute, that they were born Muslim, not converts. Just saying this for them meant that somehow they were more authentic. On the other hand, I have heard many of the immigrant Muslims say that converts to the religion are better than they are because they were Muslim by circumstance, and converts are Muslim by choice. They recognized that there is quite a difference in being a Muslim by circumstance and being a Muslim by choice.

I have personally developed a very good relationship with immigrant Muslims, and I think this is because my wife and I taught their children in the Sunday school for a few years. Subsequently, they really got to know us well. As a result of our commitment to the children in the school, they really show us a great deal of respect. But in the beginning, when some of the children would go home telling their parents about something they learned in class, we were challenged. The child would come to class the next week and say that his mother said this, or his father said that we were wrong.

I would go right to the Qur'an and give them chapter and verse, or would go to the *Hadith* (report) and give them the dalil (proof). After this happened a few times, the families would come back to us, apologizing and accepting that we knew what we were talking about.

There are still things that come up because most of the immigrants follow a particular school of thought. They follow it blindly and will rarely go against that school even if they are shown that in this particular situation they are wrong. This is a conflict that needs a lot of work, but I think we will be able to convince them, over a long period of time, that what we are saying is correct. We will be able, in my opinion, to convince them that even their Imam said to accept a *Hadith* that may contradict his words.

This is a very strong point that was stated by each of the four great Imams that most of these immigrant Muslims follow. However, I have found that it is hard to get people to change. People who have believed in something or believe in a certain way very rarely change, unless, of course, they really value truth.

We are truly creatures of habit. Whatever was taught by family is what molds and shapes a person. One lives within this molded life for the rest of his or her life, never thinking that there could be something wrong with the teaching. This, in fact, makes one suspicious of someone who comes with a different mold.

My struggle is to continue to be patient with the community as I teach Islam not bridled by cultural context. Patience is actually challenging because there is a contextual reality to everything. Nothing is done outside of some context. I say this echoing the words of Farid Esack, "Without a context, a text is worthless."[22]

As Muslims, we all adhere to the Noble Qur'an and the authentic Sunnah of Prophet Muhammad. As correct as this statement is, it is important to understand that the text of the Qur'an and the Sunnah came in a historical context. This context was that of the Prophet Muhammad and his compatriots in the Arabian Desert. However, every people have their own context in which the Qur'an and the Sunnah need to assimilate. Esack says it this way; "The meaning assigned to a text by any exegete cannot exist independently of his or her personality and environment. There is, therefore, no plausible reason why any particular generation should be the intellectual hostage of another, for even the classical exegetes did not consider themselves irrevocably tied to the work of the previous generation."[23]

I teach Islam in the context of our American life. This is where we live and this is the 21st Century, which means that we have a lot more at our disposal than those who came before us. Yes, they are our righteous predecessors, but they were not infallible! For example, I can remember speaking to a Muslim who happened to be a Pakistani. I was talking about the Imam that he follows, Imam Abu Hanifa (who happens to have the largest following of Muslims, especially from South Asia). I mentioned that the Imam had made some mistakes. When I said that, the brother began to look to the sky thinking that something would fall on us for my making that kind of statement.

I am dealing with people who are stuck in a school of thought and who are not willing to venture out. Esack tells us, "To understand the Qur'an in its historical context is not to confine the message to that context; rather it is to understand its revealed meaning in a specific past context and then to be able to contextualize it in terms of contemporary reality."[24] This informs me that if we want to grow as an Islamic community here in America, we have to consider where we are and absorb the Qur'an and the Sunnah in our own contextual reality. Our past should be looked at as a guidepost and not a grave in which we should be buried.

---

[22]   Farid Esack, *Qur'an, Liberation & Pluralism, an Islamic Perspective of Interrligiuos Solidarity against Oppression,* (Oxford, England: Oneworld Publications), 1997, 63.

[23]   Ibid.,62.

[24]   Ibid.,61.

I must admit that it would probably be much easier to work with one culture or ethnic group, but this is not my reality; and I do not think the Creator would want it to be this way. We are a multi-ethnic and multi-cultural community, and I believe this is the way it should be. Therefore, I accept the challenge. It then becomes my awesome responsibility to break down the barriers of racial, cultural, and ethnic tension that tend to exist within our community.

We often hear it said, "Islam transcends race, ethnicity, and one's culture," (this has become a cliché). Of course this is the ideal situation, but in reality it does not exist. The reality is that race, ethnicity, and one's culture or national origin really does matter. Racial prejudice has been a problem for a very long time, all around the world.

Islam is a religion that is supposed to break the cycle of prejudice and discrimination, but it has not done so.

Professor Sherman A. Jackson has written about the Arab and Non-black Muslims who have been afflicted with race and color prejudice.[25] This is what Muslims do not talk about, but it is absolutely important if we are to ever progress as Muslims in our community. As an African American, I know that racism and prejudice can be overcome. We have been working to overcome it for years in this society, and to some extent we have been successful. There is no doubt that it still exists; however, it is mostly institutionalized. There are many Caucasians and African Americans who have gotten beyond racism and prejudice. I believe, for the most part, that those who continue to display it are few in number.

I myself am a product of the Nation of Islam.[26] I grew up under its racist teachings but have since embraced the universal message of Islam, and it is inclusive of everyone. I live in an area where it is commonplace to see African American men with Caucasian women and vice or versa. There is quite a bit of race mixing in the Mid—Hudson Valley. People have gotten beyond ethnicity.

When looking at the society in general, this seems like the norm, but not in Islam. Race and ethnicity are still powerful barriers that keep Muslims apart. I remember a Pakistani woman wanted to marry an Arab man, but her parents were dead set against it. Because the woman was educated in one of our universities (and had kind of broken away from the cultural hold of her parents), she decided that she was going to marry this individual no matter what her parents felt. My wife and I were invited to the *Neekah* (wedding) that was being held in Albany, New York. We

---

25   Sherman A. Jackson, *Islam and the Blackamerican Looking Toward the Third Resurrection*, (New York: Oxford University Press), 2005, 106.

26   Nation of Islam is the group that was started by Elijah Muhammad in the 1930's. It was a black separatist organization that taught the Blackman is G-d and the Whiteman is the Devil.

went and observed the faces of the woman's parents; they were visibly disturbed. The Imam, understanding the situation, gave a beautiful talk on what true Islam is all about. He spoke about how important it is for us to get a mate that is a practicing Muslim, and how race and ethnicity should not play a part in this at all. He stated that these were two good Muslims who had decided they wanted to live their lives together, and they should be given that chance. It was indeed a beautiful, insightful sermon.

Bernard Lewis did an historical inquiry into *Race and Slavery in the Middle East*, and clearly showed that although most would say Islam is egalitarian, this is more theory than reality.[27] The couple that I just wrote about was married eight years ago. My wife and I were recently informed at the *Eid ul Adha* (feast of the sacrifice) prayer service by the daughter's parents that she gave birth to twin boys. The maternal grandparents were beaming with pride! The family came to accept that there is nothing wrong with two people coming together from different ethnic backgrounds, and that this is what the Prophet Muhammad taught for over 23 years.

I am aware of another situation where a young Pakistani woman feared that she would never get married because of her parents' prejudice against other ethnic groups. I have personally witnessed Arab men marrying Caucasian Christian women rather than marrying African American women. I can recall speaking to a Muslim brother from Afghanistan. He wanted to marry a Muslim woman from Germany, And his family told him that if he did, they would never speak to him again. They did get married and the family did not speak to him for a whole year. The couple had a little girl and the family is now accepting the relationship.

This, in my opinion, is very questionable behavior; it speaks to the deep-seated biases and prejudices that people have. It goes against all that we have been taught in Islam. Even the late, great Malcolm X spoke about the beauty in Islam that transcends race, ethnicity, and culture. I believe, had he lived longer, he would have seen that racial prejudice also exists in the Middle East. Although it may not be as vivid or outwardly expressed as it is manifested in the U.S. it does exist.

Lewis' book definitely shows that prejudice existed in the Islamic community. This prejudice was even displayed in literature and art. Blacks were made fun of in terms of their blackness, thick lips, wooly hair; so much that even black poets spoke badly about themselves. An early poet named Abu Duluma (d. ca. 776) made fun of his own appearance; he said, "We are alike in color; our faces are black and ugly, our names are shameful."[28]

---

[27]   Bernard Lewis, *Race and Slavery in the Middle East an Historical Enquiry,* New York: Oxford University Press, 1990, 85-102.

[28]   Ibid., 30.

Seyyed Hossein Nasr made this observation, "It is important to note that in Islamic society slavery was not equated with racism. Turkic slaves became military commanders and kings and leaders, as did some black African slaves. Moreover, there was a great deal of intermarriage, and usually a slave's descendants would sooner or later melt into the general texture of society."[29]

It is clear to see that it did not start out that way, but the infectious disease did begin to spread. Nasr mentioned the slave's descendants finally becoming accepted. He did not mention it had to go three generations deep. For many, a convert is not as good as the son of a convert. A son of a convert is not as good as a grandson of a convert. Nasr continues,

> There were, of course, Arab slave traders in Africa as well as European ones, but despite the fact that European colonial powers made the presence of Arab slave traders an excuse to colonize Africa, there has never been a Harlem or Anacostia in any Islamic city. Even where there is a strong Black African presence, as in Arabia or Morocco, there is no feeling of racial distinction. Today in any grand Mosque in Morocco, at time for prayers one see worshipers ranging from Black Africans to blue-eyed Berbers, but one does not have a feeling of racial heterogeneity.[30]

It is clear that Nasr does not see that racial issues are prevalent in the Islamic community. What he says sounds so good. It is, however, not true. I have made Hajj twice, once in 1990 and then again in 2000. Both times I witnessed the poorest people being the African Blacks in the streets begging the Hajjis for money. Lewis also stressed that Arabs would not allow their women to be married to black men.

There is enough evidence to clearly show that prejudice existed, and many of the leading authorities at the time had harsh things to say about black people. The great historian Ibn Khaldun even said things that I am sure he would regret having said today. He is reported to have said, "Therefore, the Negro nations are, as a rule, submissive to slavery, because, [Negroes] have little [that is essentially] human and have attributes that are quite similar to those of dumb animals, as we have stated."[31] Aristotle, as well as others, purported that some people were by nature fit for slavery.

As one can see, this issue of race and prejudice runs deep, even though, one will certainly find those who continue to deny the existence of such. I think Barrett

---

[29]   Seyyed Hossein Nasr, *The Heart of Islam, Enduring Values for Humanity* (New York: HarperCollins, 2004), 182.

[30]   Ibid.

[31]   Lewis, 53.

and Jackson both agree that it exists. Prejudice and bias have been a problem in the Islamic community for a long time, and it has kept the Muslims from really coming together as one united community. Muslims have to first identify that this is a serious problem existing amongst us, and begin to do work to eradicate it from our community. Muslims must not continue to be in denial about this, for in order to solve this problem, it has to be identified and then worked on.

The problem did not start in America; it did not start with chattel slavery. During the Prophet Muhammad's time racial prejudice raised its ugly head. One of the companions, by the name of Abu Tharr, had an argument with Bilal Ibn Rabah (a freed slave). He told Bilal that he was the son of a black woman (this was meant as a derogatory statement).

Bilal told the Prophet about this; the Prophet confronted Abu Tharr and told him that he still had some of the *Juhiliyyah* (days of ignorance) in him. Abu Tharr realized he was wrong. He was so full of remorse for what he had said to Bilal that he lay down on the ground and literally begged Bilal to step on his face. Bilal, of course, being the type of person he was, would not do what Abu Tharr suggested. Bilal got down on the ground next to him, kissed his forehead, and told him that he loved him.[32]

This is just one of many accounts that show prejudice existed. It is said that, in early Islamic and pre-Islamic times, the Arabs looked down on the sons of slave mothers, regarding them as inferior to the sons of freeborn Arab mothers.[33] How can anyone say that prejudice did not exist in the Prophet's time? The Prophet was aware of the prejudice and spoke out against it.

He married wives from different ethnic groups to show that it was in fact a good thing to do. Maria Al Qubtiya was one of the wives of the Prophet. She was a Coptic Christian, her father was a Coptic, and her mother was of Greek origin. The Prophet also married Safiyya Bint Huyayy from the tribe of Bani Nadir from the Children of Levi (Israel).[34]

It is extremely painful to speak about the ugliness that existed among people who are hailed for having an egalitarian religion; a religion that is rooted in the equality of all human beings, a religion which is supposed to transcend race, ethnicity, culture, nationality, class, etc. It is important, however, to point out these weaknesses so that we may be able to overcome them and make the above statements a reality.

In looking back at this disappointing chapter in Islam's past, one can see that it cast a reflection on why things are the way they are today. Although African

---

[32]   Muhammad Husayn Haykal, *The Life of Muhammad* Translated by Ismail Ragi A. Faruqi, (Indianapolis, IN: American Trust Publications), 1993, 260.

[33]   Lewis, 89.

[34]   Haykal, 376.

American Muslims are no longer enslaved, African Americans continue to be treated unequally. African American Muslims continue to be looked down upon as being inferior or not quite the Muslim that one is who was born into Islam. Even the convert's children, who in most cases are born into Islam, are still looked upon as not being authentic. In other words, a convert is not better than a non—convert. A convert's child is not better than a non—convert's child.

In 2008 King Abdullah allowed a Black Imam to lead the prayer in Mecca. All applauded this; but the Prophet Muhammad had liberated the Black man over fourteen hundred years ago; therefore, for this to happen two years ago shows that something indeed was lost.

Muslims have to climb the steep hill to make our practice of Islam pristine and pure like the Islam practiced by Prophet Muhammad. Muslims must do all they can to bring into fruition the true beauty of Islam the Islam that transcends race, ethnicity, culture, class, and anything else that they could come up with to make Someone feel superior and others feel inferior.

I submit to you that Tawheed is the way to do this; it is the way to overcome the challenges we face. It is the way to come into full compliance with what our religion dictates. This cleansing will only come as a result of Muslims being totally immersed in the concept of *Tawheed*.

CHAPTER 3

TAWHEED AS THE THEOLOGICAL CONCEPT

Over fourteen hundred years ago, Prophet Muhammad in the Arabian Peninsula promulgated the doctrine of the oneness of G-d called *Tawheed*. This doctrine has been the rallying force of Muslims ever since. There is not one Muslim, regardless of whether he or she is Sunni, Shiite, or Sufi, whether in America or any so-called Muslim country, that would deny the reality of *Tawheed*. This unique concept of oneness is significantly the single most important concept needed to build solidarity between the African American Muslims and the immigrant Muslims in our Islamic community.

Tawheed is the Arabic word for the Oneness or Unity of G-d. According to Dr. Abu Ameenah Bilal Phillips, "*Tawheed* literally means unification (making something one or asserting oneness). It comes from the Arabic verb *wahhada*, which means to unite, unify or consolidate."[35] When we relate this term to G-d, it means that G-d is one alone without partners. For Muslims this is pure monotheism. When one understands *Tawheed*, it is understood that G-d is one and creation is one. We are a part of His creation and therefore we are one. This concept is supposed to shape a person's thoughts and cause him or her to recognize that the authentic identity for the Muslim is Muslim identity. This identity is more important than any other consideration. When Muslims embrace this concept, the effect is oneness of brotherhood. When a person's eyes are focused upon the oneness of G-d it guides the individual to the oneness of the community.

When Prophet Muhammad introduced this concept first to the Arabs and then to the world, the Arabs were immersed in polytheism. The Arabs believed in many gods, and they even had replicas made of the gods they worshiped. This concept of one G-d was revolutionary. It caused quite a stir among the Arabs, especially because

---

[35] Abu Ameenah Bilal Phillips, *The Fundamentals of Tawheed* (Islamic Monotheism, Riyadh, Saudi Arabia; Tawheed Publications, 1990), 1.

it represented a concept of G-d that was unseen, yet G-d had dominion over the heavens and the earth.

Those who embrace this concept are known as Muslims (those who submit their will to do the will of G-d). The concept of *Tawheed* is broken down into three aspects, not to be confused with the Christian Trinitarian concept. These three aspects have been given to Muslims in the form of a catechism to make it easier to understand. According to the tradition, Arabs had no problem grasping the concept as it was expressed to them in a language they understood (Arabic). Muslims from other lands whose language was not Arabic were given the message in a lesson form.

The first aspect of *Tawheed* is called *Tawheed ul Ruboobiyyah*. This means maintaining the unity of Lordship. Only G-d has the right to be called *Rabb* (Lord). G-d alone is the one who nourishes and sustains life. As Muslims, we must understand this aspect completely, giving all homage to G-d as the one who nurtures us and all His creation to its completion. This is the Creator/Sustainer quality of G-d. G-d is the cause of all things. He is the one who sustains and maintains creation without having any need from it or for it. He is the Lord of all the Worlds (all systems of knowledge). There is no power or might except His.

The Qur'an gives us many verses to support this. One particular verse states: *"Allah created all things and He is the agent on which all things depend."*[36] When Muslims fully internalize this concept, it is understood that all power is in the hands of the Lord of all the worlds, and no one else has a share in this. Each mosque is seen as the house of G-d. Therefore, we come to that house to worship Him, and we recognize ourselves as one voice, one social community, under one command, the command of G-d.

The second aspect of *Tawheed* is called *Tawheed ul Uloohiyyah*. This means maintaining the unity of worship. Only G-d has the right to be worshiped. When maintaining this aspect of *Tawheed*, it is important to not allow ourselves to be overtaken by anything in society that would come between our Lord and us. It is clear that the polytheists worshiped many things as god. They worshiped the sun, moon, stars, trees, etc. For Muslims, nothing has a right to be worshiped besides G-d. This means not bowing down to money, women, men, homes, anything! One may ask how this trickles down into the lives and actions of Muslims. We worship the Creator. We believe we are worshiping the real G-d. There is no other one but Him. In terms of dealing with worship, people worship what they give a lot of weight or attention to in their lives. It is that on which they place more importance. Sometimes it is in fact G-d, and sometimes it is other than G-d. Many Muslims say they worship G-d, but in reality they worship customs, race, culture, ethnicity, class, and status. These "things" come between them and their pure devotional worship of G-d.

---

[36] Qur'an, 39:62.

The third aspect of *Tawheed* is *Tawheed ul Asma Wa Sifat*. This means maintaining the unity of G-d's Names and Attributes. This aspect allows for Muslims to appreciate various qualities of G-d. It introduces Muslims to learn many of G-d's Names and Attributes. Muslims become acquainted with ninety-nine Names of G-d. The understanding is that we can only call Him by what He has called Himself or His Prophet Muhammad has called Him. We are also to understand from this aspect that we are to accept His Names and Attributes and their meanings without changing or twisting the meaning.

We are also informed that if we take on the attributes, we must put the prefix *Abd or Abdul* (slave or servant of) before the attribute. G-d is *Al Rahman* (which means the Merciful Benefactor or Most Gracious). This is the name for G-d alone; if a person has this attribute as a name, that person must be called *Abdur Rahman*. These Names and Attributes really speak to G-d's qualitative nature, and to know them puts the Muslim in a very good position.

I have taught the concept of *Tawheed* many times to new Muslims, and one of the questions I ask is what Attribute of G-d resonates for them? My wife has said without hesitation that Allah is *Ar—Razzaq* (The Provider). Allah will always provide what you need when you need it. Therefore, having knowledge of the ninety-nine Names and Attributes of G-d will fortify one's faith and trust in G-d.

The person who crystallizes these three aspects of *Tawheed* into their lives will stand upon the strongest foundation in Islam. This person will be a pure monotheist and will know of a surety that there is none like unto Him. "He is one alone without partners," "neither begetting nor being begotten," and is "absolutely eternal."[37]

In laying out the concept of *Tawheed* in its various manifestations, it is my hypothesis that if Muslims truly understood the *Tawheed* concept there would be one solidified community, not a community fragmented by cultural, racial, national, or ethnic identities. It would be quite a unique community, one community with one unifying identity, the Muslim identity. This would be in spite of the differences of culture, race, nationality, or ethnicity. It is my belief that Islam came to eradicate these other types of superficial considerations.

In Prophet Muhammad's last sermon, he stated, "There is no superiority of an Arab over a non-Arab or a White over a Black, superiority is in obedience to G-d."[38] This was his last major address to over 100,000 of his followers. The question is why would the Prophet mention that there is no superiority of White over Black or Arab over non-Arab if there was not an existing problem in the community? I submit that

---

[37]   Qur'an, 112:1-3.

[38]   Muhammad Husayn Haykal, *The Life of Muhammad*, translated by Isma'il Ragi A. Al Faruqi (Indianapolis: American Trust Publications, 1993), 486.

it was because he knew of the problems existing and did not want them to become worse over the years. This makes good sense to me. The Prophet addressed the problem himself as only he could.

The Prophet also said in this famous speech, "Those who are present take this to those who are absent, for perhaps they may understand it better than you."[39] These words, in my opinion, stress a very important point, which says that Muslims in the future may understand or make more sense out of what the Prophet said than those who were in his presence. It speaks to Muslims being able to embrace his message of *Tawheed* (unity), unhindered by cultural, ethnic, national or racial considerations. In no way am I suggesting that this is an easy task; however, because we are creatures of habit, the way we were brought up is usually what we continue to perpetuate.

G-d tells us in the Qur'an that the best among us are the ones who are regardful[40] to G-d, the ones who are most regardful of their duty to G-d.[41] It does not say the one who was born a Muslim or the one who is from Pakistan or India or Morocco or America. It does not speak about race or ethnicity. It speaks about action—moral action, righteous action, being in compliance with the Lord of all the worlds. Constantly conveying this message to people would hopefully get them to see that it is important to actively respond to their Muslim brothers and sisters in an Islamic way. Any other way could cause harm and strife and would obviously be unIslamic.

When one fully grasps the concept of the oneness of G-d, he or she realizes that this oneness should act as a catalyst to bring Muslims together regardless of race, ethnicity, culture, or national origin. What we have found in many Islamic communities is that Muslims are separated and divided. Muslims have not come together to be that one united community under the concept of *Tawheed,* the very message that Islam, under the Prophet's tutelage, was meant to foster. Instead, what we find are Muslims aligning themselves with people from their own countries, e.g., African Americans with African Americans, Pakistanis with Pakistanis, Arabs with Arabs, etc.

The Prophet Muhammad recited words from the Qur'an that he said is the word of G-d. Those words were, *"We were created into nations and tribes so that we would get to know one another."*[42] When Muslims truly get to know one another, recognizing that we are all one united community, the false barriers that have been erected as wedges between us will disappear once and for all. Muslims will really (in my

---

[39] Ibid.

[40] In translating the word *Taqwa* Imam Warith Deen Mohammed has taught that it is more than Fear of Allah, it is being regardful. This regard is a sacred respect, and a sacred regard. The G-d Conscious person is regardful of their duty to G-d.

[41] Qur'an, 49:13.

[42] Ibid.

humble opinion), be following the pristine example of Prophet Muhammad and not following him in any superficial way.

Simply put, Muslims will have realized the ideal—unity in oneness and practice. The true unity of G-d will be practiced by the true unity (oneness) of the Islamic community. The effects of such a community will be felt around the world. I believe this is a real possibility because our community is multi-ethnic and culturally diverse. Our community can and will realize itself as the model Islamic community when it begins to fully realize and appreciate the concept of *Tawheed*.

As a Muslim, I truly believe that G-d is one and humanity, which is created by G-d, is also one. We are one with creation. G-d created us to get to know each other, not despise each other. The concept of *Tawheed* speaks to this oneness. G-d is absolutely eternal; the word for this is *Al-Samad;* it literally means "an immovable and indestructible rock, without cracks or pores, which serves as sure refuge from floods."[43] This informs the wide-awake Muslim that our foundation must be built upon this rock if we indeed want to be successful. After all, *Tawheed* is about unity, it is about unifying ourselves under this fundamental concept.

To really bring home the point about Tawheed and its importance, I have chosen the following instructive comments by five scholars. These scholars highlight several important aspects of Tawheed. These aspects are worth remembering, namely the nature of unity (Vahiduddin), its implications (Siddiqui), its significance or signifying power (Hammed), its social impact (Irving), and its dimensions (Ezzati).

In the encyclopedic Survey of Islamic Culture Vol. 1 (Islamic Theology) edited by Mohamed Taher, scholars have been brought together to collaborate the importance of *Tawheed by* emphasizing the points made above.

V. Vahiduddin speaks about what unity looks like in his essay on *Unity an Islamic Perspective,* "It will be a very vacant concept of *Tawheed* to think that this unity is the negation and rejection of idols only. It is the negation of all ultimacy to anything but G-d."[44] Vahiduddin believes if one truly understands *Tawheed,* then they recognize that this unity has to be expressed in the way we deal with each other, not in just how we see G-d.

> The concept of Unity in Islam works at three levels, the human level, the cosmic level and the divine level. On the human level, the apparent divisions through color and race, through language and status become immaterial. Mankind is divided ethnically and named differently so as

---

[43]   43 Fazlur Rahman, *Major Themes of The Qur'an* (Biblotheca Islamic, Minneapolis, MN), 1990, 11.

[44]   V. Vahiduddin, "*Unity: An Islamic Perspective,*"in Encyclopedic Survey of Islamic Culture vi Islamic Theology ed. Mohamed Taher, (Anmol Publications, 1997), 60.

to enable men to recognize one another in their specific character. Nay, even the division between the believer and the unbeliever is an integral part of the order, which is willed by G-d, and any attempt to reduce the multiplicity into a monolithic world order is doomed to failure. Mankind is one, traceable to one source.[45]

Once again, we see that the main idea is the Oneness of G-d being also expressed in the oneness of His creation. Tazimuddin Siddiqui writes about the implications of unity in his essay on *Tauhid—One of G-d*, "*Tauhid* is derived from *wahdahu* or *wahid* which means that G-d is one without a second, without any other co-eternal entity, of complete supremacy, unrivalled, unopposed, unequalled, and unchallenged."[46] I really believe that deepening the knowledge of *Tawheed* in its many layers of meaning can and must guide the Muslims of the Islamic community to aspire to become a unified community, gradually overcoming the differences of race, ethnicity, class and culture. My responsibility is then to be the agent who brings about the solidification of an inter-racial, inter-ethnic, international center where boundaries are broken and respect is shared in every direction inside the congregation.

Siddiqui continues, "G-d, the Creator, is one and from His unity follow, as a necessary consequence, the unity of Creation, the unity of man, the unity of life and universe. Thus all human beings belong to one universal brotherhood."[47] He mentions, "The belief in the universality of Divine Unity is an integral part of Islamic faith."[48] It is absolutely the crux of the matter. This is the foundation of our belief. Therefore, it must be explored thoroughly if we are to truly benefit from its meaning. Siddiqui further states, "*Tauhid* explains that G-d has no caste, community or race. All human beings are His subjects."[49] All human beings are under the authority of G-d. Siddiqui continues,

It is from the concept of *Tauhid* that we can deduce the existence of a harmonious world order, the purposive cosmos, the equality of sex and race, the equal freedom in socio-economic spheres and religious tolerance. *Tauhid* is not only a religious faith, or one's own concern to G-d as ultimate source of salvation or protection in the world and in the hereafter, but it is also the very principle of social equality. The entire mankind was one

---

[45] Ibid., 62.

[46] Ibid., 67.

[47] Ibid., 71.

[48] Ibid., 72.

[49] Ibid., 74.

community. Later on, G-d Himself made the variety of nations, not to
conflict and clash with each other, but to know one another . . . [50]

The idea is that from the one come the many, and then the many come back to
the one. This idea of oneness is not to do away with our differences; on the contrary,
it is in spite of our differences. There is dignity in being different; however, our
differences should not become a wedge blocking our respect for the differences
that are G-d-giving.

Hakim Abdul Hameed speaks about the real significance of Tawheed, showing
it as a sign for all human kind, a kind of social unity in his essay on *Tauhid and Adl:
A Discussion.* He states in no uncertain terms, "It must be admitted that the Muslims
themselves have not taken the ideas of *Tauhid* very seriously though it is impossible
to think of Islam without it."[51] If Muslims took *Tawheed* seriously, the Muslim
community would not be splintered. The Muslim community would be the model
community about which the Qur'an speaks. Hameed suggests, "It is significant to
note that *Tauhid* is not considered by the Prophet as an exclusive asset of Islam but
held to be the heritage which belongs to mankind, as a whole and a lost principle
which needs to be restored."[52] A lost principle that needs to be restored says that
something very important in the life of Muslims is missing. According to Hameed,
the concept of *Tawheed* is not fully grasped by those who claim it.

> It is the denial of parochial and regional loyalties which warp the vision of
> man, and make way for particularism, which is the denial of a humanistic
> ideology based on a vision of the oneness of the universe. There cannot
> be any cosmopolitanism worth its name which is ready to accommodate
> tribal and national loyalties and which allows them to override humanistic
> considerations.[53]

Yes, we are from different races, ethnicities, and cultures, but this should not
make us think that we are better than anyone else. We are truly part of the human
family. Therefore, humanistic considerations should precede anything else. Hameed
says, "Once the idea of oneness becomes not only the theoretical commitment but
is converted into action, the possibility of the idea of unity of mankind becomes
a reality."[54] The idea is that social unity does not exclude social diversity. There is

---

[50]   Ibid.

[51]   Ibid., 77.

[52]   Ibid., 79.

[53]   Ibid.

[54]   Ibid., 82.

unity in diversity, and recognizing this in the concept of *Tawheed* is essential for our growth as a unified community.

T. B. Irving says it best; he really speaks to G-d being the uniting factor in his essay on *G-d's Oneness*. He states, Islam is a monotheistic and Unitarian religion. It is the belief in the oneness of G-d which brings in social unity despite the diversities in human beings of different races, and different geographical inhabitants."[55] Our religion begins with having an appreciation of the oneness of G-d. We recognize that everything has to come to that reality. This is the central idea. Irving continues, "G-d is thus the factor which unites the universe out of its diversity."[56]

Dr. Abdul Fazl Ezzati is the fifth scholar whose words are helpful in linking it all together. He makes the point that *Tawheed* should shape how we walk, shape how we think and how we operate in speaking about *Tauhid* (in the booklet, Concept of Leadership in Islam)

> Islamic doctrines are not theological doctrines, only to be believed in. They influence Muslims' thinking in all spheres and fields. The Muslims' notion of G-d's Oneness *(Tauhid)* must be reflected in their own striving towards a coordination and unification of nature and man, religion, politics, faith and science, of the cosmos and man; and of various aspects of human life. The position of Islam in this respect (complete harmony and perfect cooperation of body and spirit, nature and man, unification of various aspects of man's life) is unmistakable.[57]

Given this understanding of the *Tawheedic* principle, the question becomes: what do we do with it? How do we crystallize the concept of *Tawheed* into our lives? As the Imam of a multi-ethnic and diverse community, it is extremely important to guide the community. Every opportunity must be taken to lay out the fundamentals of *Tawheed* as clearly as possible. This is done weekly at the Friday services. The times that Muslims get together for the daily prayers are yet another opportunity to speak about the various aspects of *Tawheed*. While sharing these ideas, the emphasis is put on translating what we know about *Tawheed* into our daily lives. Once again, this is easier said than done because so many Muslims are stuck in the quagmire of cultural traditions.

---

[55] Ibid., 120.

[56] Ibid.

[57] Dr. Abdul Fazl Ezzati, Article On the Concept of Leadership in Islam, Titled Tawhid, from a booklet put out by the Dawah Academy International Islamic University, Islamabad-Pakistan in collaboration with the Islamic Teaching Center (ISNA), Plainfield, IN, August 3-28, 1992 (Second regional leadership training camp for Dawah workers), 9.

It has become clearer and clearer to me that I have to get the Muslims more involved with coming to the mosque to learn their faith rather than just coming for prayers. This is the reason that we began to call the mosque "The Islamic Learning Center of Orange County." We wanted the emphasis to be put on learning. Too many Muslims are walking around with a distorted concept of Islam; some are walking around with no true understanding of Islam at all. Some people think that because a person was born a Muslim that means they have a better understanding of Islam, and this is certainly not true. I have come in contact with Muslims from the Soviet Union who had no knowledge of Islam beyond the knowledge that they are Muslim. It was against the law for them to practice their religion. They could not read the Qur'an or study their religion.

I have talked to many Muslims from other countries that do not have real knowledge of the religion, even though many of them have memorized the entire Qur'an or great portions of it. They know how to perform the rituals (although in many cases even these are not done correctly) but real knowledge of the religion is absent. This, of course, does not mean that they will not occasionally portray that they do have knowledge. Although they may be ignorant of real knowledge, they still sometimes display arrogance.

The serious student of Islam is able to recognize that such knowledge is shallow or the understanding of the religion is very superficial. It is recognized that there is some deep-seated misunderstanding of the religion that has come from ethnic and cultural traditional sources. These traditions have no basis in Islam, yet they are practiced as if they were authentic Islamic traditions. Muslims are told that matters of the Islamic religion have to be substantiated by the Qur'an and the Sunnah. This means every practice that is called an Islamic tradition must be supported with evidence from the two sacred sources: the Qur'an and the Sunnah. Those practices that are not supported by Qur'an and the Sunnah would be considered *Bidah* (a new religious innovation). We are not to add anything to our religion, yet people do it all the time.

This is why it is so important to get the right understanding of the foundation of our religion. The scholars in Islam call this *Aqeedah* (correct belief). It begins with the correct way to appreciate the Creator. This gives the person a solid foundation in terms of the concept of *Tawheed.*

I submit to you that, in reality, to reach this ultimate goal, Muslims will have to make a concerted effort; but it is such a beautiful concept that it will be worth all the effort. This is the reason I am using my ministry setting as the ideal place to bring this universal concept into fruition.

CHAPTER 4

COGNITIVE RESTRUCTURING—
THE THEORETICAL CONSTRUCT

The Ministry project was started because I identified a problem of divisiveness existing in the Masjid. In order to eradicate the problem, I introduced the concept of *Tawheed*, as a catalyst to bridge this divide for the young people selected for this project. I believed that the young people would be more amenable to change, and transitioning would be possible, utilizing a particular theoretical construct.

This theoretical (psychological) construct is called Cognitive Restructuring (challenging belief patterns). The belief is that people behave a certain way based on a set of core beliefs (be they correct or incorrect). The idea is that if you can change the attitude (thinking), you can change the behavior.

On giving an explanation of Cognitive Restructuring, C. Reddick states, "Cognitive Restructuring or challenging belief patterns do not focus on behavior. It focuses on the thoughts driving the behavior."[58] He further states, "Cognitive/behavioral programming helps the person to understand what she thinks about herself and how that type of thinking exacerbates the problem in the first place. When that issue is addressed we can begin to expect change." This concept is within the reality therapy mode, and is concerned with thoughts, perceptions, and beliefs. It deals with thinking patterns that have been reinforced since one's birth. It clearly shows in my opinion, how one's behavior is driven by his or her beliefs.

I truly believe that knowledge comes first and then is followed by action. This belief is central to my Islamic faith, and the Cognitive Restructuring model supports my point of view. Evidence of this particular model put into action, is within the New York State Department of Corrections. In its desire to be more pro-active, the department has put more emphasis on re-entry programming for inmates soon to be released (within four months of their release). They have incorporated, within

---

[58]   http://qwcinc.com/Reddick/WorkingWithinCognitiveProgramshtm.

their program, a phase called "Breaking Barriers." This program supports the idea that if you can change the attitude (thinking) you can change the behavior.

Gordon Graham is the author of a book central to this program's approach, and he suggests that there are four educational values in this Cognitive Reality Model that are essential for understanding it. (Note: Cognitive Reality Model and Cognitive Restructuring both speak to the same concept.) They are:

1. Change is possible.
2. Current reality is a result of the beliefs, habits, and attitudes that we adopted in the past.
3. Our future is determined by our beliefs, habits, and attitudes that we adopt today.
4. It is possible to choose our beliefs, habits and attitudes in order to reach our visions.[59]

In Cognitive Restructuring, we start from the premise that change is possible and then begin to work on those things that need to be changed. By doing so, we may change our behavior. In working with the young people selected for this project, several images (see appendix C) were shown, and they were asked, "What do you see?" Varying points of view were expressed. We wanted the students to see first hand how one's perception might be distorted. This idea of presenting images is central to the Cognitive Restructuring model. These images show how a person's perception could be distorted by what has been nurturing it for a long time. Using these images is a less aggressive way of getting people to recognize how they are viewing something. Rian Mc Mullin believes that it is essential to use these images in trying to change someone's perception.[60] In using this strategy with the students I decided to use the five principles that have to be in place to help people to change; they are as follows:

1. Willingness—the students must be motivated to see things in new ways. The images that were shown helped the students to see that there was indeed another way of seeing things. You can tell a person all day long about a particular attitude or behavior; however, when you let them see it for themselves, the point is made.
2. Guidance—they must have someone to guide them who has seen the new view. This principle is very important because the students are being

---

[59]   Gordon Graham, *A Framework for breaking Barriers—A Cognitive Reality Model.* Gordon Graham & Company, Inc. Bellevue, WA 2000. iii

[60]   Rian E. McMullin, *The New Handbook of Cognitive Therapy Techniques,* New York: (W.W. Norton & Company), 2000.

directed by the teacher. I must show them that I am able to see the images that I want them to see. When the students see that you are confident in what you see they will believe that they too can gain confidence.

3. Flexibility—they must be willing to try different strategies. They must step out of the box, as it were. Everything we taught was taught with this idea in mind. We wanted the students to be free thinkers, and we wanted them to know that things are not always what they appear to be.

4. Time—Change takes time, but you have to stay with it. It took time for a particular habit to be formed; and it takes time to change that habit. The idea is to stay in the race no matter what. The change that we are looking for in our students and the community takes time, and it is hard to measure; however, over time it can be done.

5. Repetition—you must keep practicing what you learned.[61] We continued to go over the three aspects of *Tawheed* with the students until they thoroughly understood the concepts. We did skits and role-playing to identify those characteristics that were detrimental to the community. The Socratic Seminars allowed the students to ask questions, and from those questions they began to see clearer what Muslims are supposed to believe and practice.

These steps were used with the students to get them to recognize what bias and prejudice is, by considering the images that they saw. The Socratic Seminars helped them to think more critically. We presented the students the correct concepts and beliefs that should be held by Muslims; these presentations were by power point, lessons taught, role-playing and reading assignments. McMullin summarizes his ideas.

> I believe it is possible to change almost any attitude, belief, value, opinion
> or even any prejudice using the above principles. Like Roy (a reference to
> one of his students), most clients are not truly stuck with any of their old
> attitudes, no matter how ingrained. No matter how deep the roots are or
> how ancient their origins, change is possible.[62]

It is my belief that utilizing Cognitive Restructuring as the theoretical construct will enable us to bring about a change in our students.

To highlight more of the theory Graham says, "In Cognitive Restructuring, awareness is the first step to long term change—this is helping a person become aware of thinking and behaviors that need changing."[63]

---

[61] Ibid., 235-238.

[62] Ibid.

[63] Ibid., 1-3.

I will argue that many of the problems discussed in Chapter 2 concerning the Islamic community are, in fact, a result of pre-conditioned cultural beliefs. The cultural beliefs can be the greatest barriers to change. Graham remarks, "Preconditioned Cultural Beliefs are ideas or concepts we hold to be true. Sometimes our beliefs are built on false truths."[64] These 'false truths' can become barriers that divide us, and keep us separated upon race, ethnicity, culture, etc. "The first step to breaking these barriers is to examine our beliefs."[65] In my project we examine pre-conditioned cultural beliefs in our Masjid to see if they are faulty, and if they are, we get rid of them by looking at and adopting alternative principles like the principles of *Tawheed* (oneness) and *Ikwan* (brotherhood). The clear argument from the Qur'an and the Sunnah states in no uncertain terms that cultural, racial, ethnic, national, or class bias and prejudice are not consistent with true *Tawheed*. Rian E. McMullin's ideas are similar writes that,

> We cannot rightly claim to have complete knowledge of ourselves unless at some point in our lives we discover what our core assumptions are. Our surface beliefs, attitudes, values, biases, and prejudices are all based on these key beliefs, and true enlightenment can only come with firm knowledge of these keystone thoughts.[66]

Once again, we see that core beliefs are the basis for attitudes and are the foundation that our values are built upon. Since these values are false, it will skew how we view the world or how we view the people in the world. If one has a core belief that African Americans are inferior by virtue of their birth, then his or her values are false and need to be changed. If one believes that he or she is better than someone else because of an ethnic or cultural background his or her core beliefs are faulty and need to be changed.

McMullin drives the point home about core beliefs when he quotes from Ruth Benedict, "From the moment of his birth the customs into which (an individual) is born shape his experience and behavior. By the time he can talk, he is the little creature of his culture."[67] This quote reminds me of that old saying about the growth and development of a person; does this growth come from nature or nurture? Islam teaches that every child comes into the world knowing nothing, and then the family begins to fill that child up with ideas that may be good or bad. The

---

[64]   Ibid., 7-1.

[65]   Ibid., 7-2.

[66]   Rian E. McMullin, *Taking Out Your Mental Trash—A Consumer's Guide to Cognitive Restructuring Therapy*, W.W. Norton & Company, Inc. NY. 2005, 52.

[67]   Ibid., 62.

Prophet Muhammad is reported to have said, "Every child is born in a state of *fitra*, and it is their parents who make them something else."[68] This *fitra* is the natural order that inclines toward G-d, and then the family takes over and fills the child with whatever they are. My father-in-law once asked me if my wife and I made our children be Muslim. I told him very simply that they eat what we eat. It is as simple as that; whatever you are in your home is what your children will take on. When they become older they may decide to be something different.

The child develops a personality that is shaped by his or her environment; the environment is the home, school, church, mosque, etc. This environment is like a womb. A womb is a place of development and growth.

No child is born racist, biased, or prejudiced. Someone and / or some environment had to feed that idea to the child's mind. The late Imam Warith Deen Mohammed stated many years ago, "Words make people; a word is anything that brings a message to the mind." My premise, therefore, is if you can effectively change how you think, you can effectively change how you behave. William James said it this way, "The greatest discovery in our generation is that human beings, by changing the inner attitude of their minds, can change the outer aspects of their lives."[69]

To reiterate, Cognitive Restructuring involves changing the way a person thinks or challenging his or her preconditioned beliefs; and does not concern itself with one's behavior (actions). It is concerned with the thoughts that drive an individual to do what he or she does. Change the thinking (attitude), and behavior (actions) can change.

It is apparent that change is a heart matter as well. What people believe in their heads is not always what they believe in their hearts. If the two (head and heart) are together, then it means that one has to penetrate that person's heart. Although this idea may seem to be abstract, I think it is actually right on target. Dr. Robert Franklyn had this to say.

> We would do well to discover Aristotle's ancient wisdom about how educators can move beyond transferring theoretical knowledge (episteme) to forming people of character. It requires three fundamental loci: knowledge, desire and practice. We can teach what is right and good and praiseworthy. Then we must insert and reinforce the desire to choose and do the right thing. But, we must also encourage and reward its practice

---

68   Sahih Muslim Vol. IV, Imam Muslim, rendered into English by Hamid Siddiqi, Dar Al Arabia Publishing Printing & Distribution, Beirut-Lebanon, 1398.

69   William James, *The Varieties of Religious Experience*, Harvard University Press, Cambridge, Massachusetts, 1985.

and, over time, the habit of doing what is right becomes deep. It becomes
one's character. Aristotle said, Excellence is not an act, but a habit. We are
what we repeatedly do.[70]

As mentioned earlier, I was bought up in the Nation of Islam, and as a result
of this upbringing I had developed hate in my heart for a race of people. When I
received correct knowledge from the true teachings of Islam, and that knowledge
went both to my head and my heart, I had to change. The hatred that I held for
a particular people could no longer house itself in my head or my heart. I had to
give it up and recognize that a race of people cannot be condemned for what their
ancestors did hundreds of years ago.

The research supports my hypothesis. We can foster change in our youth using
these strategies. Freire clearly shows that one must gain knowledge first and then
must act on the knowledge received. Freire is working with people who have been
oppressed. He educates them about their condition and they begin to change. He
states, "It is only when the oppressed find the oppressor out and become involved in
the organized struggle for their liberation that they begin to believe in themselves.
This discovery cannot be purely intellectual, but must involve action, nor can it be
limited to mere activism, but must include serious reflection, only then will it be a
praxis."[71]

Once again the people have to be made aware that they have been thinking in
a way that is unproductive. According to Freire, once you wake the person up they
begin to change.

> Time and again peasants have expressed these discoveries in striking ways
> after a few hours of class: one person who sat in the class said, "I now
> realize I am a man, an educated man. We were blind, now our eyes have
> been opened. Before this, words meant nothing to me; now we will no
> longer be dead weight on the cooperative farm. I work and working I
> transform the world.[72]

The person's life has new meaning or has meaning for the first time, because they
are able to see that they are somebody, contrary to what they were told in the past, or
how they were treated. It took that word to start the process of change. Freire again
states, "To surmount the situation of oppression, men must first critically recognize

---

[70]   This was an address given at the annual conference of the council of foundations in
Atlanta Marriott Marquis Hotel, Monday May 4, 2009.

[71]   Paul Freire, *Pedagogy of the Oppressed*, Herder and Herder New York, 1971, 52.

[72]   Ibid., 14.

its causes, so that through transforming action they can create a new situation, one which makes possible the pursuit of a fuller humanity."[73]

To critically recognize is to speak about having deep knowledge of something. The person is made to see how they got into the pitiful condition they find themselves in. This is what happened to African Americans who were brought to America to be slaves. They were broken and denied anything from their past. They were made Negroes and had no sense of where they came from or who they even were before they were made slaves. Once they were taught (given knowledge), they began to realize that someone put them in this situation to keep them deaf, dumb, and blind. Now they are aware of who they are and that slavery is not their plight by virtue of their being born black; they in fact recognize that they are dignified human beings.

Freire states, "As long as the oppressed remains unaware of the causes of their condition they fatalistically "accept" their exploitation."[74] Freire establishes that true reflection leads to action. Freire supports my premise that knowledge comes first, and then action follows. The idea is gaining the knowledge first and then putting that knowledge into practice.

McMullin speaks about a concept called Quantum Leaps.[75] Although he recognizes that it may take a long time for people to change, he acknowledges that there are quantum leaps (the change in people almost overnight, because of being impacted by some knowledge).[76] This is very important in our project because we are looking for some change in a short amount of time. Mc Mullin agrees.

> While the overwhelming majority of clients followed this pattern (ie, taking a long time to change, my words), some clients made dramatic changes. In a few days time they changed a way of thinking that they had held for most of their lives. It was as if while climbing the mountain they suddenly jumped to summit—making a quantum leap.[77]

He mentioned a student who had gone out to a revival meeting, leaving that meeting never returning to drugs or other destructive things.[78] Mc Mullin has convinced me that images really work. He states in no uncertain terms, "These pictures are the best analogy I have found to explain a complex principle of

---

[73]   Ibid., 31.

[74]   Ibid., 51.

[75]   Ibid., 232.

[76]   Ibid.

[77]   Ibid.

[78]   Ibid., 232-233.

psychology. They are my Rosetta Stone to understanding cognitive change and growth. I believe they explain how clients make quantum leaps.[79] I have made my own quantum leap and believe that it is possible to get others to do the same.

To sum it up, the challenge for the congregation in Newburgh is to overcome its divisiveness by embracing the concept of *tawheed* in all its dimensions. To this end, it will be demonstrated that by utilizing Cognitive Restructuring as the theoretical construct, change is made possible. The twelve students will change as a result of the new knowledge they are exposed to in the six-month project held at the Mosque.

---

[79]   Ibid., 234.

CHAPTER 5

THE MINISTRY PROJECT

To begin, I first examined how Cognitive Restructuring would affect the planning stages. The concept of Cognitive Restructuring was the lens used to guide me in formulating this six-month project. By utilizing the educational values in Graham's Cognitive Reality Model, I set out to prove that by applying the concept of *Tawheed*, change is possible. The method I used was to first disseminate knowledge, as it is important for a person to garner new information before change can occur. According to Graham, current reality is a result of the beliefs, habits, and attitudes that one has adopted in the past. This reality applies to the youth who were selected to participate in this project. They came with their own pre-conditioned beliefs and attitudes, obviously something that they learned from their parents. Graham also says that one's future is determined by his or her beliefs, habits, and attitudes that are adopted today. Therefore, it is possible to choose our beliefs, habits, and attitudes in order to reach our vision. It is my assertion that once a student's biases are exposed and examined, his or her belief system will change.[80]

I also utilized Mc Mullins's five principles that need to be in place in order to help people change. In brief, they are: a willingness on the part of the participant to change his or her perspective; a teacher's ability to guide the students to the new point of view; a student's ability to be uninhibited and willing to try something new; a tenacious attitude on the part of the student; and finally, the need to continuously practice what has been taught.[81] With these tools in hand, we started our project.

---

[80]   Gordon Graham, *A Framework for Breaking Barriers—A Cognitive Reality Model.* Gordon Graham & Company, Inc. Bellevue, WA 2000. iii

[81]   Rian E. McMullin, *Taking Out Your Mental Trash—A Consumer's Guide to Cognitive Restructuring Therapy,* W.W. Norton & Company, Inc. NY. 2005, 235-238

Our exciting six-month project began on Sunday January 11, 2009. This project began with twelve eager young people, six boys and six girls. The gender, ages and ethnic backgrounds are as follows:

Girls		Boys	
Khadijah	17 Moroccan	Abdur Rahim	15 Moroccan
Fatimah	16 Moroccan	Yusuf	15 African
Samirah	15 Trinidadian	Bilal	13 African American
Aisha	14 Pakistani	Uthman	15 Pakistani
Aliyyah	13 Bangladeshi	Jamal	15 Bangladeshi
Sana	13 Puerto Rican	Akbar	14 African American[82]

As was mentioned in the previous chapter, this project was started because the writer identified a problem of divisiveness existing in the Masjid. I believed that in order to eradicate the problem we would have to work with the young people who are more amenable to change. The following is an overview of what took place month by month with the young people at the Masjid.

Step #1: Defining Project Objectives

The students were informed that for six months we would be working together to analyze the relevance of race, culture, and ethnicity in Islam.

They were told that the premise behind this project was to discover whether or not we should allow differences to continue to divide us or should we find ways to allow our differences to unite us. (The students overwhelming agreed that their parents were the ones with the superiority issues, and they would love to "teach them a lesson.") We then listed the following behavioral objectives:

1. The students will be shown several images and these images will be used to show how one's perception can be distorted, and how one can change that perception.
2. The students will learn about *Aqeedah* (correct belief) and the three basic principles of (*Tawheed* (oneness of G-d).

---

[82]   In keeping with the agreement made with the student's parents, and also protecting them, I am not using their real names. I am however, using their gender, ages and ethnicities.

3. The students will learn about the significance of the Qur'an and Sunnah and the role each plays in guiding a Muslim's life.

4. The students will demonstrate their understanding of *Aqeedah* and *Tawheed* via Socratic seminars, student-run discussions, assessments that contain both objective and written questions, a culminating product-based project that includes building the Kaaba. (Note: The building of the Kaaba was changed to building an ideal Islamic community. The reason will be explained in detail later on in the chapter).

Step #2: Discovering Students' Interests

Using a Product Planning Guide created by Joseph S. Renzulli, founder of The Multiple Menu Model, the students answered a series of questions that helped us understand where their interests lay. My wife and co-teacher, Fonda, and I quickly learned that more than half of our students preferred the hands on approach to learning. Under Renzulli's Product Planning Guide, "Models/Construction Products," most students preferred to build or create the following constructs: learning centers, buildings, houses, blueprints, and play facilities. Other preferences from Renzulli's list were his "Spoken Products, which include: speeches, debates, organizing groups, and being a part of discussion forums. Finally, a handful of students preferred his "Performance Products" such as: viewing films and videos, role—playing and creating simulations. With this information in hand, we began formulating our six-month lesson plan. [83]

Step #3: The Teaching Plan

After defining my project objectives and learning where students' interests lay, I put in place a six-month plan of action. This plan is as follows: During the first month, I plan to introduce students to the concept of *Aqeedah*, which is correct Islamic belief. This would be followed by an introduction to *Tawheed*, which is embracing the oneness of G-d. During the third month, students will perform their

---

[83] This product planning guide was created by Joseph S. Renzulli, who is the founder of the multiple menu model is the approach we used as we identified the different styles of learning of the students, having already been aware of the concept of multiple intelligences. It was adapted from Renzulli, J. S. Leppien, J. H., and Hays, T.S. (2000). The Multiple Menu model, Mansfield Center, CT: Creative Learning Press.

understanding of *Tawheed* in a skit. The next month, we will visit other faith groups to learn how we are all connected to the oneness of G-d. During month #5, we will watch, for the second time, the film on the *Hajj* to see if students understand the profundity of this season and its representation of the oneness of G-d. Finally, students will construct an ideal Islamic community and explain, to the community, how *Tawheed* can impact us all.

Month #1: Introducing the Concept of *Aqeedah*

We evaluated students' benchmarks and discovered their understanding of unity. To this end, a series of questions were asked. Then we had them fill a pouch and put what they thought was valuable inside it. After that, we showed the film on Hajj. For the next few Sundays, we used various reference books and other materials, and our students were introduced to the idea of *Aqeedah* (the correct Islamic belief). (The pouch is explained in detail later on in this chapter.)

Month #2: Introducing the Concept of *Tawheed*

For *Tawheed* (oneness of G-d), Fonda developed a power point presentation entitled "Applying *Tawheed* in Today's Society." After the presentation, students were asked to choose a random piece of paper out of a box. Each slip of paper had a role they played. For example, one slip of paper read: I am a biased Pakistani who despises Bangladeshi people. Another one read: I am a disgruntled old woman who believes a woman's role is to stay at home with her children. While half the students role-played, the other half were the analytical audience who applied the principles of *Tawheed* to each situation. We spent a lot of time with the three aspects of *Tawheed* because we wanted to make sure the students really grasped the concept.

Month #3: The Performance and Celebrating the Gift of Differences

During the third month, students worked diligently to bring their new-found understanding of *Aqeedah* and *Tawheed* to our Islamic community. Parents were invited and watched a 45-minute performance. The skit, "Uniting Together as One" was received well with a lot of open-ended dialogue following. The students' performance clearly expressed the importance of embracing *Tawheed*. (The entire skit can be found in this chapter.) In addition, students shared their cultural differences, by bringing in a meal, or some other example, to show that our differences are to be celebrated and not despised. Another way differences were celebrated was in the viewing of the DVD entitled, "African Americans and Islam."

Month #4: Visiting Other Faith Groups

For a month of Sundays, various faith groups visited our mosque, and we reciprocated the visits. We visited both a Christian church and a Jewish synagogue. Students discovered common threads between us. One Sunday, during a visit from a local temple, a sixteen-year old boy made a very poignant comment that will stay with me for a very long time. He said, "I am glad I listened to my Rabbi 'cause he told us your beliefs were very similar to ours. I didn't know you guys believed in Abraham and Isaac." It is my belief that inter-faith relations connects us as one. Although there may be some differences, our commonality is much more important.

Month # 5: Viewing *Hajj* on Film

The students viewed the documentary film on *Hajj*, again. Students showed that they could readily see the ultimate, "coming together as one," event. For homework, students prepared for an upcoming Socratic Seminar. They developed questions relevant to the *Hajj. One student asked,* "If my parents really have correct belief (*Aqeedah*) in their hearts, why do they think they are better than people with darker skin?"

Month #6: The Culminating Event—Building an Ideal Islamic Community

Students were asked to build, what they believed to be, an ideal Islamic community. Using various materials, students simulated a Muslim community, with *Tawheed* as the nub of its existence. This mosque, built in the center of town, was named "Masjid *AT-Tawheed*." Note: Initially, our plan was to build the *Kaaba* because it symbolizes the ultimate coming together of all Muslims during the Hajj season. However, due to varying viewpoints amongst community members, we halted this project. Some members thought we were creating religious innovations by building the Kaaba. The doubters believed that since there is only one *Kaaba*, it is an insult to try and simulate another. As a result of the above confusion, we went to a Plan B as outlined above.

The Project

Understanding *Aqeedah* and *Tawheed* (months 1&2)

We worked with twelve young students who were eager to participate in the six-month project. The project started out with a focus group. We asked a series of questions about the meaning of *Aqeedah* and *Tawheed*. We discovered that our students did not have a clear understanding of what *Aqeedah* and *Tawheed* are. We informed them of the concept and also how important it is to Muslims who are really trying to practice their religion. We also asked about the relevance of race, culture, ethnicity, national origin, etc. We talked about whether or not they had a real place in the Islamic community. We showed the students some images to illustrate to them how easy it is for a person's perception to be off.[84] The students saw a series of pictures; one in particular was of a young woman and an old woman. Some of the students couldn't see the young woman, and others saw the young woman and couldn't see the older woman. We told them it is all about perception. Sometimes your perception is right, and sometimes your perception is distorted. When you look at others and think you are better than they are, this is an example of a distorted perception.

The discussions were very thought provoking. During the discussion another bias was bought out, that of gender. The students spoke out against the biases that they see in the Islamic community as it relates to women. This observation came from the female students, and it became crystal clear that there are other concerns that we should all become aware of that are also divisive.

In setting the foundation in the class, we established very early that Muslims are supposed to be guided by the Qur'an and the Sunnah. If there is a statement made or a position taken, as it relates to Islam, one should be able to substantiate the same by identifying a proof (*dalil*) from the Qur'an and/or Sunnah. The following statement from the Noble Qur'an supports my thesis on unity

> O humanity! We have created you from a male and a female, and made you into nations and tribes, that you may know one another. Verily, the most honorable of you with Allah is that believer who has At-Taqwa (one who is G-d conscious). Verily,
> Allah is All Knowing, All Aware. Noble Qur'an 49-13

The aforementioned verse was given to the students in a Socratic Seminar. The question was, "What do you think this verse means?" Answers varied. Some thought

---

[84] Rian E. Mc Mullin, *The New Handbook of Cognitive Therapy Techniques*, New York: (W.W. Norton & Company), 2000, 218-232.

the verse was speaking about the first man and woman others thought that the message is about our differences, as well as our sameness; and finally someone said that it also points out who is in fact the best from amongst us. One student asked what the *Tafsir* (commentary) has to say about the verse? This point expressed that the student did not want to just give her opinion, she wanted the *Dalil*. I shared the following *Tafsir* with the students to show them that they were right on target.

In explaining this passage from the Qur'an, Sayyid Abul A'la Mawdudi provided this insightful contemporary commentary

> In the verses above, the Muslims are provided with the necessary directives to keep their community immune from evil and corruption.
>
> But now through the present verse mankind is being warned about the major erroneous notion that has always led to the spread of evil around the world; namely, the notion of prejudice based on race, color, language, homeland and nationality. Addressing all human beings, the Qur'an emphasizes three basic points:
>
> 1. That all human beings have the same origin, that all of us have arisen originally from the same father and mother. Thus, all ethnic and racial entities that exist today are branches of the same human family, their ultimate parents having been the same.
> 2. That it was natural for mankind to become divided, despite their common origin, into diverse national and tribal entities. While this diversity is quite natural, it does not provide any justification for some people to claim any inherent superiority over others; to consider some on these grounds as high and others low, some as noble and others as people ignoble.
>
>   Consideration of color, race or nationality do not warrant of any particular color, race or nationality to regard themselves as superior to others. G-d created such diversities to foster greater cooperation and to enable these different entities to become mutually introduced.
> 3. There is only one basis for regarding one as better than the other and that is on account of their moral excellence.[85]

These verses are not ambiguous, they are very clear. There are many others that were shared that need not be repeated here. The point is made; Allah speaks to creating all humanity from a male and a female—Adam and Eve. He also

---

[85]   Sayyid Abul A'la Mawdudi, *Towards understanding the Qur'an* published by The Islamic Foundation United Kingdom, 2006, 1065-1066.

speaks to making the people into various nations, and tribes. This implies that we are all different, and this is exactly how Allah wants us to be. It also speaks to the importance of getting to know each other. This getting to know each other is not in any superficial way, it is knowing about people's culture, ethnicity, etc. The verse goes on to speak about the best person being the one who is most regardful of their duty to G-d. This lets us know that race, culture, ethnicity, national origin, and class etc. means nothing to G-d. G-d is all Knowing and All-Aware.

In our youth class, Yusuf stated that if G-d created us to be different, then there is nothing wrong with being different. Aisha agreed, but indicated that our differences should not be a wedge between us. We should be able to celebrate our gifts of difference in a way that enhances everyone. After this discussion, it was decided that we would have each student come to class and display their culture in dress, food, and or artifacts. We thought by doing this it would really show appreciation for each other's culture. It would enhance the student's awareness of the "other." The students were very excited about the prospect of celebrating their cultures. This part of the project will be discussed more in detail a little later in the chapter.

A National Geographic DVD entitled, "Inside Mecca" was shown to the students. This 60-minute program showed three pilgrims making the Hajj in the Holy City of Mecca. It showed the trials that they all went through, and it captured the spirit of the Hajj. To go on Hajj is an absolutely wonderful and spiritual experience that is not truly appreciated from reading about it. To read about it only gives you some glimpses of its reality. To actually see it taking place right before your eyes is only second to going there yourself. The use of this powerful visual aid is very instructive.

It is important to see that this approach (using the DVD) fits the hypothesis that knowledge comes first and then action. Knowledge comes to us in many different ways. It is not always the spoken word; it may be the spoken word along with pictures. Or it may be a visual aid such as a T.V. show or a DVD. It is processed in the mind as real knowledge. In a discussion with a professor about the knowledge coming first and then the action, the professor mentioned that people had knowledge about the perils of chattel slavery; however, it did not really come alive for many people until they saw the series called *Roots*. When they saw *Roots* it drove the point home because this was real knowledge in the form of a powerful visual aid called T.V. The use of power point presentations, You Tube, films, movies, smart boards, etc., are just more tools utilized to make the point. It is still knowledge being presented. Even a play or a musical sends a message to the mind.

As noted earlier, Imam Warith Deen Mohammed said, "Words make people, and a word is anything that sends a message to the mind."[86] The recent T.V. news

---

[86] Imam Warith Deen Mohammed, Statement made in a speech given in Chicago in 1975.

concerning the earthquake in Haiti was just such a "word" that affected people. The commentator made the point that the devastation caught on the screen really made people see how tragic the situation was. The people would not have been able to get the real picture from articles in the paper. Just imagine, people sitting in the comfort of their living rooms looking at their 52-inch flat screen T.V. The sight of the devastation is enough to make people shake with fear! Rabbi Sacks says, "The image speaks louder than the word. Images evoke emotions."[87] There is greater impact from the images than from the mere word.

After viewing the DVD, we formed a Socratic Seminar and questions were asked. One question was what excited you about the DVD? Khadijah said, "Seeing all those people from all over the world together in one place." Uthman asked, "Why were the men all dressed in two pieces of white cloth?" I explained that this was part of the ritual garb. The men are the leaders in the society and some are rich and some are poor. All the men standing before G-d must take off their cultural dress and show sameness, not difference. This is one of the beauties of the Hajj. Akbar said, "The Hajj is an expression of the unity of humanity." Samirah said, "If the Hajj expresses unity of humanity, why are we so disunited?" Bilal said, "Because we allow our differences to get in the way." My wife Fonda said, "All of our differences, be they culture, race, nationality, etc., should not be dividing barriers." I mentioned that people do not quite understand that Tawheed should unite us, not divide us, and this is why we are here in this class. We want to bridge this artificial divide. Aliyyah said, "Even on the Hajj there was some display of bias against the South African man and also the Caucasian female Muslim." I told her that people go on Hajj but they bring their biases with them. The hope is that the people submit themselves to Allah and get rid of all those things that are not a part of Islam. Overall, the comments and the questions were good. The students all said they enjoyed the DVD. They said they learned a lot from it.

I decided to give them a little more information about the Hajj. I shared some words from my spiritual leader, the late Imam Warith Deen Mohammed.

> The Hajj is symbolic of triumph or victory for religious people.
> As you know, Islam is a religion that recognizes all the great Prophets of Almighty G-d, from the very earliest prophet to the last Prophet Muhammad.
> That includes Moses and Jesus, the Christ. The Hajj is the sign that G-d is going to give victory to those prophets who struggled and prayed and served G-d so that the human being would come into the right spiritual

---

[87] Jonathan Sacks, *The Dignity of Difference—How To Avoid The Clash of Civilizations*, Continuum, New York 2002, 3.

life—would come to high moral standards, and would come to believe in
the oneness of G-d and the oneness of humanity. So the Hajj is symbolic
of the victory for the religious people. One G-d, one creation, one
humanity.

When we visit the Hajj, we go there in one dress. Oneness seems to prevail
throughout all the steps of the Hajj. We wash first; all of us wash the same
way.
We have a ritualistic kind of way that we wash called ablution. We put on
the Ihram, the two pieces of white linen cloth, and the women, they dress
all the same in garments covered from their heads to their feet. Strangely, it
seems the women are allowed to wear regular dress as long as it is covering
the head and the whole body, but men, can't wear their nationalistic dress.
We can't go in our American suits and the Pakistani can't come in his
Nehru suit, the African can't come in his famous headpiece with ropes
around it. Nationalism and arrogance come from men in leadership and
not from women leadership.

So Islam abolished all artificial barriers that separate man from man and
society from society. The Hajj is the strongest symbol that we have in Islam,
of that oneness.

The Hajj doesn't recognize any superiority of male over female. As you
know, in social life—that is, in the community life—the male is the Imam
(leader) in the religious society. An Imam means, he takes the lead. He
goes in front of the congregation, he leads the congregation. But, when we
go to Hajj or make Hajj, we circle the Kaaba and we pray. You might find
women praying in front of you. That demonstrates that actually, there is no
spiritual, moral or intellectual superiority given to male over the female.
That the male and the female are equal in this sense. During the Hajj,
all of the artificial status and power status, class distinction and positions
of authority and whatnot that have been formed are all abolished. And
racism is one of those artificial class statuses (something that preserves)
for certain people over others, and that is abolished.[88]

After sharing these notes with the students, I spoke about my own unique
experience of Hajj. I told the students that I actually went on Hajj twice; the first
time in 1990, and then again in the year 2000. I mentioned that I could attest to

---

[88]   Imam Warith Deen Mohammed. Article on *The meaning of Hajj*, 1975.

what Imam Warith Deen Mohammed said about the men wearing the two pieces of white linen. All the men looked the same. You could not tell who was rich from who was poor. You could not tell what country people were from.

The high point for me was that all the people were there for the purpose of pleasing G-d—fulfilling the rituals of Hajj, and it was, in my mind, the single most expressive act of testifying to the oneness of G-d. I also appreciated the fact that many of the standard ways that we practice our religion at home were suspended on the Hajj. For instance, I recalled praying behind women and no one making a fuss about who should be where. Women traditionally are to be behind the men; however, when the *Athan* was called it was so crowded in the Masjid that you could not move. When it was time to pray, you prayed where you were, and it was totally acceptable.

This showed the equality of both men and women. The rituals are not restricted to just men, both practice the rituals. Another observation was the women who wear the *neeqab* (face veil) could not wear it during the Hajj, they must take it off. I distinctly remember in the year 2000 when my wife and I went on Hajj with a group of fifty people. In this group, there were ten couples, and out of the ten couples seven of the women wore *neeqab*. They wore it traveling to the Holy City, but once they started the pilgrimage they had to take it off, and I saw their faces. The main point I made is that during the Hajj everyone; men, women and children practice all the rituals. We all do the same thing.

Once again, I asked the students if they had anything they wanted to say, and Sana said, "The Hajj makes the case for us all being one human family, and I wish that the spirit of the Hajj was expressed by Muslims all the time." I agreed, along with the rest of the class (who were nodding in agreement). I said this is a very important statement, and it is our responsibility to get the word out to the people, starting with our own families. I told the students they should share this information with their parents.

Fonda said, "The Hajj experience really made me see how important it is to respect everyone, no matter where they come from, whether they are male or female. Everyone is part of the human family and is honorable and dignified. How could anyone go on Hajj and then go back to wherever they have come from and not be changed for the better?" I mentioned the only way a person could come back not a changed person would be if they were merely going through the rituals of the Hajj, and had not allowed it to become a part of their souls. Dr. Shamshad Ahmad illustrates this point even further.

> The Prophet made it clear in his last sermon how we are to be and how
> we are to treat people. I had read this sermon in the past many times, but
> listening to it in its original atmosphere, and in the sea of humanity of
> about four million devotees, all standing and supplicating, was entirely a

> different thing. It shook me inside, and I saw that it shook others too. Our
> imam repeated this sermon after we finished the afternoon prayer outside
> of our tent in Arafat. We all cried. With a trembling heart and shaking
> body, I made a resolution and promised the almighty that I would try my
> best to follow the prophet's sermon in letter and spirit. I have violated his
> teachings since then often. May the Almighty forgive me.[89]

It really takes a concerted effort to stay focused and to practice Islam as it should be practiced. This means that you accept all Muslims as authentic and do not discriminate against Muslims because of their race or color. This is a perfect example of a person recognizing how he should behave but falling back into habitual behavior as it relates to treatment of other Muslims.

I informed the students that we would revisit our talk on the Hajj and that we would have a simulated Hajj right at the Masjid. We would build a *Kaaba* and go through the rituals of Hajj so that they would get a better feel for it. Unfortunately we never did get a chance to build the *Kaaba* because of time constraints and the resistance from some of the members of the Masjid who thought we would be doing something wrong if we did this. Some thought that it would be introducing a religious innovation to the community, and we have been warned not to introduce anything new. They did not understand that this would not affect the religion at all.

It was merely a way of educating the children by having a hands on approach to a ritual that they would one day, hopefully, fulfill. Rather than cause friction, we decided not to build the Kaaba. Instead, we just showed the DVD again and had the students write a paper after having a Socratic Seminar about the Hajj. As I think about it more now, I believe we should have done something more to symbolize the Hajj. Even if it was only putting on the two pieces of cloth to see how it felt, something more tangible should have been done. I will make sure that we do something more in the future.

The next few weeks my wife and I taught on *Tawheed*. This was very important because it is the very foundation of this work. My premise was that the concept of *Tawheed* is the catalyst that will bridge the divide between immigrant and African American Muslims. We introduced the students to the three aspects of *Tawheed*, *Tawheed ul Ruboobiyyah* (unity of Lordship), *Tawheed ul Uloohiyyah* (unity of worship), and *Tawheed ul Asma Wa Sifat* (unity of Allah's names and attributes). These three aspects were gone over thoroughly earlier in this book. Along with teaching them

---

[89]   Shamshad Ahmad, *Rounded up Artificial Terrorists and Muslim Entrapment After 9/11*, The Troy Book Makers, Troy, New York, 2009, 207.

the principles of *Tawheed* we taught them about diversity and the problems associated with prejudices, biases, racism, and discrimination. Each one of these discussions ended in Socratic Seminars. The students really enjoyed them because they got a chance to ask a lot of questions. We showed them clips of *Muhammad the Messenger of G-d* (a film on various aspects of the Messenger's life) that dealt with character development and comments concerning Islam's stand against racial prejudice, and its stand for equality and justice. The students participated in role playing to identify how wrong racism, biases and prejudices are. The students showed that they clearly understood that racism, prejudice, biases, and discrimination have no place in Islam. When it does exist in the community, it is because the people have allowed their race, culture, ethnicity, nationality, language, or social status to cause them to erect artificial barriers. The students learned that race problems or problems of prejudice exist in various religions, as well as cultures of the world. They realized that it definitely exist, in our own religion although it should not, if we truly hold on to the pristine concept of *Tawheed.*

A very important point that was made with the students was how the schools in Saudi Arabia are very proficient in teaching the subject of *Tawheed*. This subject comes under the title of *Aqeedah* (correct belief or creed). The idea is that in order to be an authentic Muslim, your *Aqeedah* has to be correct. If you say you are a Muslim, and you say that G-d is a man, then your *Aqeedah* is off. If you say that G-d is a spirit, your *Aqeedah* is off as well. If you say that G-d is everywhere, this too is an incorrect statement and your *Aqeedah* would not be right.

There are six elements to the Muslim belief system: Belief in Allah, belief in His Angels, belief in His Books, belief in His Prophets, belief in the Day of Judgment, and belief in preordination. The first belief is the one that speaks about *Tawheed.* Unlike the five pillars of Islam, the articles of faith (the belief system) are not action oriented. These beliefs are not practiced, they have to be studied. You have to study the beliefs to increase your faith in Islam. Therefore, to really understand the concept of *Tawheed* you have to study. In studying the three aspects of *Tawheed* the students learn that to say G-d is everywhere is to say that He is in everything, and G-d is not in waste or corruption . . . Our teaching tells us that Allah is above the heavens, above the throne, in a way that befits His Majesty. Allah is everywhere by His knowledge.

In order to get the students to really appreciate what we were saying, we gave them each a stringed pouch. We told them that the pouch was to be used to put their valuables in. In fact, the word *Aqeedah* has its roots in a pouch that the Arabs used to carry their valuables in. This is the beauty of the Arabic language; it is rooted in the earth. You can find something tangible as a root of many of the words.

As we taught the aspects of *Tawheed,* we asked the students to write down on a small piece of paper what they thought was valuable to them. When the students were asked to share what they put in their pouches, we saw pieces of paper with the words family, brothers sisters, cell phones, I pods, T.V., etc. The pouch was something physical, but it represented something not as tangible—the heart. The pouch represents the heart that is the place where you keep your valuables—what we believe in and hold dear is in our hearts. The students got it because they held the pouches in their hands, and they continued to put things in them that were valuable to them.

As we continued to teach on *Tawheed,* the students began to write on pieces of paper; Islam, Allah, Prophet Muhammad, various attributes such as *Al Rahman, Al Rahim, Al Malik, Al Quddus,* etc. It was indeed a fun project and the students showed that they gained a lot from it; they also took a quiz on the attributes (see appendix D).

The students learned that Allah is the only one who has a right to be called Lord, as He is the cherisher and sustainer of all the worlds. They learned that Allah is the only one who has a right to be worshipped, and that Allah is named what He has named Himself, and what Prophet Muhammad has named Him. They also learned that no one has the right to twist or change the meanings of G-d's names to suit him or herself. The point was clearly made that if a person recognizes and appreciate the oneness of Allah then he or she should recognize and appreciate the oneness of all of creation—the oneness of humanity.

The students also understood why it was so important not to see G-d in fleshly form. The idea of G-d being in the flesh automatically excludes others from the equation. If G-d is black, whites are excluded, and if G-d is white then blacks are excluded. We were able to show the students how a whole race of people were told that G-d was white, and the angels were white, and all that was right was white. They were able to see how this would cause some people to have an inferiority complex and others to have a superiority complex.

Each of the students had to write a short essay on the Islamic perspective on racism; the following is Aisha's essay:

> I feel that racism/prejudice in Islam are two conflicting ideologies. A true Muslim could never be racist. The existence of racism in Islamic nations and societies is due to cultural beliefs, not religious. The racist thoughts that some Muslims have are not coming from their religion, but from other parts of their personality. Some people say that we are all a little prejudiced. This might very well be true because we all grow up in different environments and are exposed to different things. Our experiences shape who we are and some people's upbringing might cause them to feel negatively towards a specific race or group. If it's true that we all have biases, then we must learn to put them aside.

I feel that throughout my childhood race was never an issue. My parents taught me not to judge people and to respect everyone. In my school I was also educated about acceptance of the differences of others. I was taught that differences were not a thing to be feared, but a thing to be celebrated. Our differences, both physical appearances and personality, make us beautiful and unique. If a person's parents are not prejudiced, then their children are less likely to be prejudiced.

Many times I have heard the phrase that we should "tolerate" differences. I think that tolerance is not something to be strived for. The dictionary definition of tolerance is: the act or capacity of enduring; endurance. When a person tolerates something they are bearing a pain. I also believe that people should not be color-blind to race, but should be race-accepting. We should be able to respect and celebrate the differences that exist between people.

We must learn to overcome differences and love one another. That's where Islam comes in. The message of Islam is of peace. Muslims are taught to respect differences. Verse 13, Chapter 49 of the Qur'an says, "O Mankind, We created you from a single pair of a male and a female, and made you into tribes and nations so that you may know each other (not that you despise each other). Verily, the most honored of you in the sight of Allah is he who is most righteous of you." This verse exemplifies the Islamic viewpoints on how to treat those of different ethnicities and nationalities. Allah has told us to understand and become acquainted with people of other races, not to dislike them. In Islam a person's skin color does not dictate their level of importance or superiority. The best person is the most pious one. If a person embraces Islam with their whole hearts, they will no longer have room for hate and racism in them. The cure to prejudice is to follow the words of Allah.

I think that Aisha really captured the essence of what we have been teaching in her short essay. It was really good to see that she used the Qur'anic verse as *dalil* (evidence) for what she was saying. Aisha said the cure to prejudice is to follow the words of Allah. I agree with her. If people followed the dictates of Allah, we would really be in good shape. The reality is that people do not, and this is why we are so divided.

The Skit (month 3)

The following is a skit that was put on at the Masjid during the third month. The name of the skit is "Uniting Together as One."

Character Names:

Khadijah—an eighth grade student. Her parents are from Saudi Arabia.
Fatimah—an eighth grade student. Her parents are from Morocco.
Samirah—an eighth grade student. Her parents are African Americans.
Aisha—a seventh grade student. Her parents are from Egypt.
Aliyyah—a seventh grade student. Her parents are from Puerto Rico.
Sana—a sixth grade student. Her parents are from Pakistan.[90]

Setting:

It is the year 2009, and six middle school Muslim girls are in their school cafeteria. These girls are planning a weekend of fun. All is peaceful until a very important conflict is revealed.

(Girls enter from various parts of the Musella (place of prayer). They are carrying lunch trays).

Fatimah:	As-Salaamu Alaikum (The Peace be unto you).
All:	Wa Alaikumus Salaam (and unto you be the Peace).
Fatimah:	How's everybody doing?
All:	Girls start adlibbing how they are doing.
Samirah:	Al hamdulillah. You know, praise be to G-d. But it's getting harder and harder to carry so many books and my lunch bag, too.
Fatimah:	Girl, I don't know why you always carrying books when it's time to eat. **(Other girls adlib their agreements).**
Samirah:	Well, you know I don't go anywhere without my books. **(She holds up her Qur'an).**
Khadijah:	But if you gonna keep carryin' them, stop complaining so much.
Samirah:	Whatever. **(Samirah puts up her hand, ignores her and starts reading and eating simultaneously).**
Sana:	Speaking of complaining. Somebody needs to complain about this food. It's disgusting.

---

[90] These are the names that we have been using all along. They are not the student's true names.

Fatimah:	Well, it's definitely not Halal and it can't be Kosher. (She lifts food up).
Aliyyah:	It's revolting!
Khadijah:	It's (spell the word) N-A-S-T-Y!
Sana:	It's a shame. All we doin' is wasting our parent's money. None of us eat it!
Aisha:	(Holding her nose). You know that's right. I'm tired of even looking at this recycled dog food!
Aliyyah:	You ain't nevva lied, girl. This food is wack!
Samirah:	**(Everyone but Samirah laughs. She holds up her lunch bag and taps it indicating that this is what they should be eating).**
Khadijah:	**Listen,** enough about food. It's Friday. Are y'all coming to my sleepover? It's gonna be so much fun and we're gonna have a **Halal** barbeque first!
Sana: Yeah,	I really wanna go!
Aisha:	I know it's going to be **mad** fun!
Fatimah:	I wanna go, but I don't know what my parents are going to say.

(All the girls, but Samirah, start adlibbing their agreements in the following order)

Aliyyah:	I can hear my mom now. A sleepover? No! No! **and** No!
Sana:	When I ask my mom, she's gonna have a fit.
Aisha:	Yeah, my mom's gonna flip!
Fatimah:	My mom's not **even** gonna wanna hear nothin' bout no sleepover!
Aliyyah:	You ain't nevva lied, girl. Let me go call my mother right now.
Fatimah:	Yeah, I'm going to call mine, too.

(All the girls walk away to call their mothers. Samirah remains reading her Qur'an. Girls return looking extremely sad).

Fatimah:	**(breaking the silence): OMG!** I can't go! I knew that meanie would say, **"No!"**
Aliyyah:	Yeah, my mother said, no, too. **(looking at Sana).** What did your mother say?
Sana:	**(shaking her head).** Surprise, surprise! **(Said sarcastically).**
Aisha:	Yeah, surprise. My mother said no, too.
Fatimah:	I don't understand. Your parents and other adults are gonna be there!
Aisha:	It has nothing to do with whether or not her parents are going to be there.
Sana:	Yeah, nothing at all.

Aliyyah:	(spoken very sadly) Yeah, you ain't never lied.
Khadijah:	I just can't believe **all** of our parents said no. What could it be?
Fatimah:	It's a shame. When are we ever gonna be able to get together **besides** at the Mosque?

(Fifteen seconds of silence. Silence is broken by a crying Sana).

Sana:	I hate to admit it but . . . (Interrupted by Aisha)
Aisha:	Wait a minute! Does your mom only want you to hang out with **"your own kind?"**
Sana:	That's it! How did you know?
Aisha:	Because my parents are the **same** way!
All but Samirah:	Mine too!
Aliyyah:	My parents have always been like this. I wonder what we can do to show them we want to hang out more.

(They all look at Samirah, who has been silently reading her Qur'an the whole time).

Samirah:	What? Why is everybody lookin' at me?
Khadijah:	Come on Samirah, help us out here.
Samirah:	Oh, now you want my help. (Pause then shrugs) No problem. **(She holds up the Qur'an)** The answer is right here!
All:	What do you mean?
Samirah:	Allah says in Chapter 49, Verse 13 " . . . He has made us into nations and tribes so that we may know one another, not despise one another . . ."
Fatimah:	(translates in Arabic).
Samirah:	Now, no parent (in their right minds) will ever debate with what G-d says.
Aisha:	That's true, but why don't our parents **already** know this?
Sana:	I don't know, but it's time they learned!
Fatimah:	Looks like we have some work to do!
Aliyyah:	Hey, you know what?
All:	Yeah, we know. We ain't nevva lied!
Samirah:	(She stands). Respected elders, honored dignitaries, brothers, sisters, and friends. We the young sisters of Masjid Al Ikhlas understand that our differences only help to make us stronger. We have made a commitment to begin to know one another. It is our hope that we will never despise one another.

(At the word commitment, all the girls stand as one. When Samirah finished, there is a group hug).[91]

Imam Salahuddin: **(from the audience yells)** "You ain't nevva lied!"

This skit, as simple as it might appear to be, speaks volumes about a problem that exists within the Islamic community, the problem of racism and prejudice. The major theme embedded in this skit is that by applying the three aspects of *tawheed*, the feeling of superiority can be eradicated. Reactions to the skit varied. Some community members were brought to tears, and some people thought we had a lot of nerve bringing this sensitive topic to the forefront. For those who were brought to tears, a lot of discussion ensued. They wanted to know how they could begin to make a change in their thinking. The Muslims who perceived the skit as being an audacious move remained silent; however, their body language portrayed anger. Overall, it challenged the vast majority of the community to think about the biases that exist and to try and make some changes in the way we treat each other.

Later that month, students shared their cultural differences. Because we wanted to explore what Allah meant when He said, "He created us into nations and tribes, that we may get to know one another," we celebrated the gift of difference. We asked the students to come to class and share something about their culture, ethnicity, language, etc., and share artifacts, dress, and/ or food. This added a nice touch to the class. It allowed the students to recognize and experience the dignity in differences. Khadijah, Fatimah, and Abdur Rahim shared some Moroccan sweets with the group. They also displayed some clothing that they wear, as well as spoke about the beauty of the country. Samirah shared some artifacts and history about Trinidad. She brought in some Trinidadian style curry chicken. Aisha and Uthman shared some information about Pakistan. They also had artifacts unique to the Pakistanis. They treated the group to *Somosa* (rectangular shaped fried dough with potato filling and beef filling). Aliyyah and Jamal shared some history about Bangladesh. They told us that because they were surrounded by water, fish was their main dish. They shared some Bangladeshi fishcakes with us. They also had some artifacts to share.

Although all the students were supposed to participate by sharing their individual cultures, we had a problem with Yusuf the African, Sana the Puerto Rican, and

---

[91]   This skit was written and directed by my wife Fonda K. Muhammad. On the most part it was well received by the parents and others in the community.

Bilal and Akbar, the two African Americans. Even though they agreed to a date that they would share; when that day came, they claimed they were unprepared. I spoke to each of them separately and tried to get them to see how important it was for them to share their culture, but they never did. I even spoke to their parents and told them that the other students, who shared, may perceive those who did not as not being happy with who they are or where they came from. Although it was disappointing, it showed that there were some deep-seated problems that they had not yet overcome. We talked about slavery and what happened to Black people to cause them not to love themselves. Although in the end, these students never shared, a lot was learned from the students who did share. The beauty of diversity, the gift of difference, made an impact on the class. The key, therefore, is to acknowledge each other, to get to know each other, to then respect each other. This means that people have to leave their comfort zones and venture into the space of the 'other.' When one experiences the 'other,' the person finds out so much that is good. It is a very rewarding experience. It is the command of G-d. As I noted earlier, Aisha said, "We should be able to respect and celebrate differences that exist between people." Those differences have nothing to do with the nature of the human being. We are all from the same human source or beginning.

In speaking about how to avoid the clash of civilization, Rabbi Sachs (chief Rabbi of the United Hebrew Congregation of Britain and the Commonwealth) advocates what he calls the dignity of difference—an active engagement to value and cherish cultural and religious differences, rather than mere tolerance and multi culturalism."[92] Even though in this case the Rabbi is speaking about different religions, the idea is the same. There is dignity in our differences. Our differences are gifts to be acknowledged, cherished, and respected. When we recognize this, our horizon is expanded. Our life perspective is deepened, and our worldview becomes more appreciative.

Dr. Jamillah Karim says, "By acknowledging and respecting differences within the ummah, American Muslims will be better able to build bridges across difference."[93]

Karim, (speaks about the Qur'anic verse that tells us we were created into nations and tribes).

> The verse acknowledges human difference based on collective identity, for example, ethnicity, nationality, and language. The ethical implication of this difference, however, is that human groups are expected to learn about one another, as opposed to remaining ignorant about one another. The

---

[92]   The Fountain Magazine, March/April 2009 edition, 51.

[93]   Dr. Jamillah Karim, *American Muslim Women, Negotiating Race, Class, and Gender Within The Ummah,* New York University Press, 2009, 236.

Arabic verb *ta'arafu* comes from the root, *'arafa*, which means, "to know, to come to know." A variation on the root, *ta'arafu* means "they became mutually acquainted, or they came to know one another," referring to a mutual process among groups. Through its root *'arafa*, *ta'arafu* is linked to the word *ma'ruf*. *Ma'ruf* has multiple meanings, one of which is "good fellowship with one's family and with others of humanity. In his commentary on verse 49:13, Imam W. D. Mohammed translated *li-ta'arafu* as "to recognize one another" and stated that this recognition implies both "knowledge" of one another and "respect" for one another.[94]

Much to our surprise, our already established Family Days helped to reshape this project. Our students wanted to stay at the mosque, after Sunday school, so they encouraged their parents to return so that they could be a part of it. This was good because, for those six months, we had some families there that would probably not have participated. When we have Family Day at the Masjid, it is an excellent opportunity for Muslims to try different types of food. Every family is asked to bring a main meal dish to share. This is a time to really get to fellowship with your brothers and sisters of faith. This coming together, breaking bread, and socializing, helps to break down those false barriers. The Masjid becomes the hub for these activities, and becomes a place that is frequented for more than *Jumu'ah* services or the five daily prayers.

Family Day is such a good idea that the neighboring *Masajid* (Mosques) have started to do it as well. They do it on different days; some do it on Sundays, and others do it on Friday evenings. This means that we can share not only at our individual *Masjid*, but we can share at other *Masajid* as well. In doing so, we get to meet even more Muslims, and share more ethnic meals and embrace other traditions.

In addition, during this month, the group viewed a DVD on African Americans and Islam. It was a new film tracing the Muslim roots of African Americans. The film talked about color-blindness, and some of the students took exception to that terminology. Some said the term used should be color acceptance and that we should accept the fact that we are a multiplicity of colors. Students said we should celebrate our differences, recognizing that we are all the same dignified, honorable human beings.

The film showed that African Americans made a contribution to the growth and development of Islam in America. They were introduced to Muslims who were bought here from Africa and made slaves in this country. The film also showed some pseudo Islamic groups, as well the contributions of El Hajj Malik Shabazz (Malcolm X) and Imam Warith Deen Mohammed. Overall, the students enjoyed

---

[94]   Ibid., 237.

the film and all of them said they had no idea that African American Muslims made as many contributions as they did. The viewing of the film allowed the students to appreciate some of the struggles that African Americans have had to come through in this country.

Visits to Other Faiths (month 4)

During this month, we visited both a church and a synagogue. Students were able to see the common thread between Muslims and people of other faiths. This was revelatory because they were also able to readily see how *tawheed* connects to the other faiths' theology. In a round-circle setting, students discussed various aspects of their religions in an informal manner. Most of the questions were prepared, but the spontaneous questions are the most memorable ones; for example, when the Jewish boy asked about our understanding of Abraham, or when the Christian girl asked about how we viewed Jesus Christ.

Viewing the *Hajj* Film (month 5)

As mentioned earlier, we showed the DVD on the Hajj, one more time, as we were not able to have the simulated Hajj. After viewing the film, "Inside Mecca," each student was told to write down some questions for a Socratic Seminar, and afterwards they were asked to write a short reaction about the film. The following are some of excerpts from their papers.

> Yusuf wrote: Hajj is a pilgrimage that every Muslim should make if they have the health and the wealth. What Hajj means to me is unity of all Muslims from different places of the world. In Hajj everybody is the same. It doesn't matter if you're rich or poor, Black or White, we're all equal.

> Abdur Rahim wrote: If you call yourself a Muslim then you are well aware of many things you must do to remain Muslim. For example, the five daily prayers, during the day. Another is to give Zakat to the less fortunate. Even more important is to go to hajj. Hajj is a pilgrimage to Mecca. In this journey a Muslim must embark on this religious experience to follow the steps of Prophet Muhammad. It is said if you do hajj correctly all your sins will be wiped away. It will be like having a clean slate. Hajj means to improve and get another chance. We can become closer to G-d mentally when we do this. It also gives us a chance to redeem ourselves.

Samirah wrote: Based on the documentary, "Inside Mecca," one can learn several rituals practiced while performing the last pillar of Islam. Not only did I learn about the rituals of hajj, but also the attire of men. The men must wear two pieces of white cloth. When they wear the two pieces of cloth it shows that people must dress simple, to show that everyone is equal. It is like the African man said, "literate and illiterate, poor and wealthy, all come together in unity." Also, everyone must be in the state of Ihram. When you're in a state of Ihram, you must be patient. As one can clearly see, this documentary on hajj helped me learn many things that I never knew before. Hajj itself is a beautiful journey and changes people who made it. Afterwards, those same people strive to become better Muslims and eliminate worldly desires. Each ritual of hajj shows the unity of millions of people present. Also, the attire of men shows a great example of how nobody is superior to anybody else and that everybody is equal. Therefore, by watching this documentary on hajj, it makes me want to make hajj even more and live in a state of Ihram.

Aisha wrote: I really enjoyed the DVD on Hajj. I wish we were able to do the simulated Hajj. I understand that we are all on different levels. What was profound to me is seeing all the people together—they all looked the same, especially the men who wore two pieces of white cloth. It was a great expression of unity, of oneness. I thought to myself I can't wait to go on Hajj. I appreciated the struggle that the White female Muslim went through, and also the African Muslim man from South Africa. I think that if you truly give yourself to Allah all of those false barriers have to give way to unity.

The young people were, in my opinion, able to grasp the meaning of the Hajj. They thoroughly enjoyed the DVD and were pretty upset about our not doing the simulated Hajj. I assured them that it was okay and that maybe one day in the future we might do it. But for now we would have to be satisfied with seeing the DVD on Hajj.

Building the Islamic Community (month 6)

In our final month, we decided to create an ideal Islamic community. We ended our six-month program by displaying this Islamic community to the students' families, and it was left on display for the entire community to see. The students did a wonderful job putting the community together. To get started, my wife took the students shopping, and they brought all kinds of materials to help them creatively develop the ideal community. There was a Masjid, a community center, a women's hair salon, a men's barbershop, a Mall, a park, and a Halal meat store. Sitting in the center of this community was the mosque. The students called this house of worship "Masjid *at Tawheed*." They wanted everyone to know that this Masjid was built on the proper foundation—the oneness of G-d.

Overall, the students depicted an Islamic community made up of different races, cultures, and ethnicities. There was a very unique building adjacent to the mosque called The Unity Building. Students explained that this building would be used to celebrate differences and to have an open dialogue between people of different ethnic backgrounds. The students talked about how they would not allow differences to put a wedge between them, but instead they would celebrate them. One might call it the Utopian society because it was ideal in every way—a community built on the oneness of G-d.

CONCLUSION

As I write this, we have just braved a serious snowstorm that touched the lives of many people. This storm did not take into consideration one's ethnicity; African Americans, Whites, Indians, Pakistanis, Bangladeshis, Africans, the rich, and the poor were equally affected by the severe blizzard. Those who live in fine houses were affected as much as, or maybe even more than, those who were living in apartments. The rich, the middle class, and the poor were without power for days. Those who could afford to stay in hotels did so. Those who could not afford hotels stayed in makeshift shelters or stayed in their own cold dark homes. The beauty of it all is most of us made it through and are now enjoying spring.

This conclusion will be broken down into two sections, one section will cover the outcomes from the project, and the other section will cover the insights for the future.

OUTCOMES FROM THIS PROJECT

Outcome #1: *Tawheed* as the Crucial Teaching of Islam Makes a Difference

The students showed that they comprehended what was taught by doing really well on the quizzes and essays they wrote. They showed they understood what is Islamic and what is not. They really showed they had a good understanding of the three aspects of Tawheed. They also fully grasped the importance of *Aqeedah* (we talked about the pouch being the place where one keeps their valuables, etc.) The students had to memorize the three aspects of *Tawheed*, as well as chapter 112 and chapter 49, verse 13 of the Noble Qur'an. Each student had to recite the verses and the aspects of *Tawheed*. They also had to articulate the meaning of each aspect along with the meaning of the verses. By utilizing meta-cognition,[95] we were able to check their understanding. This measure was used to make sure they fully grasped the concept. We asked questions like how is racism viewed in Islam? The students had to give their evidences from the Qur'an and the Sunnah to support their

---

[95]   Meta-Cognition is checking the thinking behind the thinking.

understanding. The students realized that in order for a person to really change they had to allow for the concept of *Tawheed* to permeate their entire being. This permeating would allow the person to recognize that every person is a part of the human family and race, culture, ethnicity, nationality, and social status do not make one person better than the next. The best of us are those who are most regardful of their duty to G-d.[96]

Throughout this book I argued that it is possible for one to overcome biases or prejudice, if they submit themselves to Allah and let the beauty of the religion take over. It is about identifying the real problem to sincere Muslims and then giving them the opportunity to change. When individuals truly understand the concept of *Tawheed*, then they do not allow themselves to be diverted by things that are, in essence, meaningless. Remember, if a change in thinking can be successfully made, so can a change in behavior be accomplished.

Outcome #2: **Focusing on These Insights Changes Behavior**

In our six-month project, we unearthed and explored so much. We challenged old beliefs and cultural norms that have no place in Islam. The students were right there with us. It became apparent that they would not have the problems that their parents had or some of their other family members. The students showed that they were not tainted. They were not going to allow their culture, race, or ethnicity to cause them to look down upon others. The students recognized that the one who is better has nothing to do with where you come from or how you look. Karim says, "Second generation, and even more often the third is regarded as the one that will overcome ethnic divisions in the American *Ummah*. American Muslims have little expectation that the first generation will correct their prejudices but have great expectations for the second generation."[97] These last few months have shown me that first generation Muslims are being confronted by their children, and they are slowly making changes. There are more interracial marriages taking place. The families have been fighting these marriages; however, the second generation is pushing forward.

We also showed that inequality and injustice were in fact expressed not only by modern day Muslims, but it was also reflected in ancient Muslim literature, arts, and folklore. We were able to clearly show the students the contrast between what Islam teaches and what Muslims practice.[98] It was shown that even before chattel slavery,

---

[96] Qur'an, 49:13.

[97] Jameelah Karim, *American Muslim Women, Negotiating Race, Class, and Gender Within The Ummah*, New York University Press, 2009, 45.

[98] David M. Goldenberg, *The Curse of Ham, Race and Slavery in Early Judaism, Christianity and Islam*, Princeton University Press, New Jersey, 2003, 20.

Africans were looked down upon because of the color of their skin. This was bought to light by some of the stories we related earlier, where the Prophet himself had to speak to the problem.[99]

I believe the project greatly impacted the community because culturally and ethnically diverse families were bought closer together, as a result of their children growing closer together. Each week, we had different family members bring in lunch for the students. We had different ethnic dishes to try, as well as good ole American pizza pie! Every first Sunday we had family day and the students encouraged their families to stay for the program. This was indeed impressive because the children are usually ready to leave after classes. As a result of our program, more parents came out to the Masjid. Although the family day is something that was set up long before the project, I believe that the project helped to get more members of the community out. This was indeed a great surprise.

Outcome #3: **Youth are open to This Approach**

The students kept journals wherein they wrote essays and some personal observations. They answered questions for deep reflection. There was class instruction, DVDs watched and discussed, power point presentations, student oral presentations, book readings and sharing of magazine articles. Role-playing and skits were a hit. It made the students really get involved in the project. Celebrating differences made the weeks very memorable. Socratic Seminars evoked thought provoking questions and helped our students delve deeper into the concept of *Tawheed*. In having discussions with some of the students' parents, they have acknowledged things are changing for the better. The students' families were happy that their children participated in the six-month program. They realized that it was full of meaningful things to do.

Outcome #4: **Through the Youth these Insights have an Impact**

As a result of our project, the youth have been encouraging their families to participate more in the Masjid activities. One recent happening is that many of the immigrant Muslims came to the Masjid after observing the *Eid* prayer in a hall filled with over two thousand Muslims. They had been used to going home and celebrating the *Eid* with their two and three generation deep families. They now return to the Masjid and celebrate with their indigenous Muslim brothers and sisters. This, in itself, is a big step in the right direction. There are all kinds of ethnic food, gifts are

---

[99]   Muhammad Husayn Haykal, *The Life of Muhammad,* translated by Ismail Ragi A. Al Faruqi
(Indianapolis: American Trust Publications, 1993), 486.

given out, and there is a spirit of love and happiness. Daisy Khan has something to say about our unity in this pluralistic society.

> Islam is neither Western nor Eastern. It is confined neither by geography nor history. There are, however, certain unique elements of Islam as practiced in the Western context. Given the traditions, singular history of cultural adaptations, of taking the best of a culture and rejecting the worst, this represents nothing novel. In the context of the U.S., I envision an authentic American expression of Islam thriving within our pluralistic society without compromising its essential values and beliefs. This "American Islam" cuts across cultural boundaries, carving an identity that combines the best of what it means to be "Muslim" and "American." I firmly believe that the core values of Islam—faith in obedience to the Divine, reverence for the individual rights and communal well-being, compassion and justice, respect for pluralism and diversity—are entirely resonant with American values.[100]

Outcome #5: Teachings Become the Leverage for Change

In our months together, we have spoken about so many things with the youth, marriage was one of them. We talked about interracial marriages, and the students agreed that it would be islamically acceptable to do so. They agreed that it should be left up to the two individuals who want to get married. The following is a short essay on Islam and Interracial Marriages written by Aisha, one of our students.

> I have never been told I must marry within my own race. Some members of my family have married interracially and everyone has accepted their choice. I am sure that if I loved someone of a different race my parents would allow me to marry them. Although I have never been told that I must marry someone of my own race, it has been implied that it would be best for me if I did. The only reason for this is that life would be easier for me if I married someone of my own race because society is generally not as accepting as my family of interracial marriages. If I married outside of my race, I would be confronted with more problems than if I did not. I would be faced with questions and I would have to deal with dirty looks from strangers. I know that people treat interracial couples this way because I have seen it happen. In everyday settings such as grocery stores, I have

---

[100]   Daisy Khan, *Balancing Tradition and Pluralism,* Sojourners Magazine, Faith, Politics, and Culture, February 2009, 15.

seen people look at interracial couples and their children with looks
of confusion. These looks are something I would rather not live with.
However, if I truly loved someone of a different race then this would be a
problem that I would be willing to deal with. I would not be discouraged to
marry someone outside of my race by family because interracial marriages
are not prohibited in Islam.

Aisha wrote about interracial marriages and what society thinks about them.
This look of confusion is disappearing right before our eyes, as is the idea of it
being wrong is steadily losing ground. People are breaking that taboo everyday.
It is becoming more and more acceptable, and in some parts of America, it is
commonplace. More and more Muslims are also breaking these taboos and getting
married to Muslims of different ethnicities. I am personally aware of cases where the
young people have decided against their parents wishes to get married.

A most recent case was a thirty-six year old Indian Muslim who wanted to marry
an African American Muslim. The Muslim man's family was dead set against it. They
came up with excuses for him not to marry her. What will people say about the
children? She's black! What are the children going to look like? What they were
not recognizing is that the woman was Muslim, and a very good one at that. They
loved each other. The man's family said they would take him to India to get him a
bride. He was thirty-six years old. That should have happened along time ago. They
even stooped so low as to tell him that if he did that it would kill his father (as he
had recently had a heart attack). To make matters worse, the Muslim man's father
seemed to really have his Islam intact. Everything was o.k. as long as his son did not
bring home a black bride. Well to make a long story short, the father and mother
finally agreed after a year and some months. They gave them their blessings which
was all they wanted in the first place.

INSIGHTS FOR THE FUTURE

Insight #1: **Low Self Esteem Can Hinder Growth in Faith**

Although the students learned a lot about the power of *Tawheed*, the project was
not problem free. The majority of the students shared their gifts of difference with
their fellow classmates. It would have been even better if the students, who did not
come forward to share their culture, had participated. They experienced the gifts of
differences from their classmates, but they themselves did not celebrate their own
racial or cultural differences.

A deeper problem surfaced as a result of some students not sharing . . . There
seemed to be some problems with love of self. The African, African American,
and Puerto Rican students appeared to be suffering from low self—esteem and a

negative self—concept. I thought about this and wondered why the students did not feel empowered by the fact that their teachers are African American. As I thought deeper, I remembered when I was a child my brothers and sisters used to call me "chocolate" because I was the darkest in the family. My mother said to me, when I mentioned my problem to her, that she and I shared the same complexion. This was true, but I did not see her. I just saw my brothers and sisters and my stepfather (who was as light as my biological father). When I was growing up, the darker skinned people were the ones picked on, and the lighter ones were more accepted in my neighborhood. This rang true for the general society as well. It could be, as in the student's case, we were too close to the situation, so they did not see us either.

Imam Warith Deen Mohammed had taught about this syndrome for over thirty years, he called it the "residue of slavery." We, as descendants of slaves, still have the residue of self hatred. Some of us do not believe that we are as good as anyone else. When I reflect back on the time that we had together during the project, I think more individual time should have been spent with those students who did not share their culture, to try to build up their self-esteem and to help them develop a more positive self-concept.

In terms of the work that was given, the Puerto Rican girl student did very well on all of her tests and quizzes. She scored higher than anyone else. The African and African American students didn't do as well. This should have been the sign that something was wrong. Fonda and I represented ourselves as positive role-models; however, the above mentioned students appeared to have low self esteem and a negative self—concept. They appeared not to love themselves. This was obviously a missed opportunity to do more to help them learn to love themselves.

True Islam can break the cycle of prejudice, racism and discrimination; however, it becomes harder to break when it is mostly institutionalized. The African Americans or people of color feel like the deck is stacked against them. They feel the racism in the society. Everywhere they turn they feel a sense of rejection. As previously mentioned, sometimes it is real, and sometimes it is not.

Insight #2: **The Divide between Ethnic Groups in a Mosque is Problematic**

Immigrants, for the most part, are not interested in the struggle that African Americans have to go through. Karim says, "By discounting the African American struggle, immigrants downplay the systemic effects of anti-Black racism and downplay immigrant privilege.[101] This is a problem. However, I have argued that if one truly

---

[101]   Jamillah Karim, *To be Black, Female, and Muslim: A Candid Conversation about Race in the American Ummah,* Journal of Muslim Minority Affairs, Vol. 26, No. 2, August 2006, 228.

submits himself to Allah, and practices Islam in its pristine purity, the problem can be eliminated. As mentioned earlier, my experience with the Nation of Islam is proof that a person can change and thereby eliminate the problem.

During my research, I came across other Muslim writers who have identified the divide between immigrant and African American Muslims. They have written much material and have acquired a huge amount of statistical data on the existing problem. However, they have not suggested a way to bridge the divide. I submit that my hypothesis provides the solution—the bridge if you will—to that divide. What I am proposing is the natural practical way to bridge the divide. Karim touches on this idea.

> Existing racial, ethnic, class, and gender divisions demonstrate that the *ummah* is not united. Over time, differences in ethnicity, language, and religious ideology have always challenged Muslim unity, but Muslims have always subscribed to the ideal of religious brotherhood and sisterhood. Although not always a reality, coming together as a community inclusive of all racial and ethnic groups is an ideal in the consciousness of most Muslims.[102]

In her paper, Karim clearly articulates the existence of the divide.

> Immigrant Muslims have a level of power, authority, and privilege over African American Muslims. This privilege is what distinguishes racism from racial prejudice. Racism is a system of advantage based on race. Beverly Tatum uses this definition to highlight the power and privilege that whites enjoy over blacks and other people of color. She boldly asserts people of color are not racist because they do not systematically benefit from racism even though they can and do have racial prejudices. As people of color, South Asian and Arab immigrants do not share privilege and power with whites. To gain acceptance among whites, however, many do participate in anti-black racism.[103]

This speaks about how the South Asians position themselves in the society to become successful, and this means they have to distance themselves from African Americans, Muslim or not. Once again, this is not something that has to exist. If we truly embrace what Allah has given us, then we cannot show prejudice toward

---

[102] Jameelah Karim, *American Muslim Women, Negotiating Race, Class, and Gender Within The Ummah*, New your University Press, 2009, 11.

[103] Jamillah Karim, *To Be Black, Female, and Muslim: A Candid Conversation about Race in the American Ummah*, Journal of Muslim Minorities Affairs, Vol. 26, No. 2, August 2006, 226.

our brother and sister in Islam just because they are from another race, culture, or ethnicity. The verse in the Qur'an that speaks about our being created differently so that we can get to know one another[104] was thoroughly explored, and it was shown that knowing each other is much more than merely acknowledging one another. It is celebrating, appreciating, and respecting each other. Thus, it allows Muslims to recognize there is unity in diversity.

My analysis is doable, albeit, challenging. Nevertheless, if truly striven for, it can and must happen. Karim even quotes from Dr. Seyyed Hossein Nasr (a well known Scholar in Islam), who says, "No segment of the Muslim community has a right to claim to be the ummah anymore than a segment of a circle could claim circularity . . . A networked epistemology thus allows us to see unity and difference at the same time."[105]

Our differences are a gift, not a curse, and Muslims have to start recognizing this and remove the artificial barriers that keep the gaps so prevalent. It is time to get past the talk and to get into the action. Once again, a Muslim activist, Rami Nashshibi (executive director of the Iman organization in Chicago) comments on this idea.

> This is your *ummah*. It is one *ummah*. Never underestimate a concept that unites beyond ethnicity, class, and race . . . It is a lofty ideal but Muslims have championed this concept for fourteen hundred years. American Muslims commonly refer to themselves as the *ummah*, but they fail to live up to the concept, post 9/11, we have no more time for slogans. We have to be real about this thing.[106]

Insight #3: **The Planned Hajj Experiment Evoked Theological Reactions**

The biggest disappointment and setback (in the project) to me was not being able to do the simulated hajj. The students were really excited, as we were about doing it; however, there was some opposition from some of the members of the Masjid against us building a *Kaaba*. The thinking was that we would be committing a *bidah* (a religious innovation—introducing something new in the religion). No one was willing to give me the help I needed to get the materials to build the *Kaaba*. Therefore, we decided to view the Hajj DVD again, and make an ideal Islamic community. This setback taught me that we will meet some resistance along the way, but we must continue to go forward, because what we are attempting to do is the right thing.

---

[104]   Qur'an, 49:13.

[105]   Jamillah Karim, To Be Black, Female, and Muslim. 13.

[106]   Ibid., 68.

I contend that Muslims have been giving great speeches about the one united *ummah*, but they have not done serious work on trying to make this happen. It is one thing to talk about the unity of the Muslims, yet another to strive with might and main to make it a living reality. I submit that it starts with individuals working on themselves, getting rid of any false ideas that are not Islamic. As Karim mentions, "Like race, ethnicity is artificial, not a fixed, marker of human difference."[107]

We are on the threshold of a new life here in America. We have people here from every part of the world.

Those immigrants, who came here thirty and forty years ago with the intent to go back to their countries, are now here to stay. Their children and their children's children are Americans who were born and raised here. If they travel overseas, it is a trip to connect to their parents, countries, but they recognize themselves as Americans. It is absolutely imperative that Muslims in America have an "American Muslim Identity." By the same token, it is equally important for the Muslims in America to bridge the divide and embrace their fellow Muslims, fully, transcending ethnicity, culture, race, nationality, etc.

The future still looks promising to me, and I am strengthened by the spirit of the young people who are striving to please G-d, unobstructed by the baggage with which their parents came to this country.

I mention this to support my belief that things are in fact changing. It is slow in some places and other areas it is happening pretty quickly. I believe that our Masjid is on the cutting edge of change; we are a multi ethnic and multi cultural community. I believe things are changing naturally because people are embracing true Islam. Having said that, we have to continue to teach and educate the people on the true meaning of *Tawheed* to allow them to shed the false notions and attitudes that have continued all these centuries to keep us divided.

During the six-month project, I tailored many of my Friday talks to the unity of G-d and Muslims, *Tawheed*, etc. Some of the brothers and sisters would come to me after the service to tell me that it was really a good talk. They would say I had made some good points, and yes, Islam transcends race, ethnicity, culture, and social status! The comments made by these congregants have confirmed for me that we are headed in the right direction.

We have within our theology the solution to our problems of divisiveness. I believe that when the baton of leadership is passed on to the next generation, they will accept it with the right attitude and right spirit. They will stand upon the pristine principles of Islam and will not be swayed by cultural or racial considerations. They will acknowledge the truthfulness of the statement that we are indeed one united community submitting to the oneness of Allah—Tawheed.

---

[107]   Ibid., 27.

APPENDIX A

Masjid Al-Ikhlas
By-Laws

Article I

By-Laws: Accepted as legal documentation by more than two-thirds (2/3's) or unanimous agreement of members being present on the following meeting days: October 2, 1988; October 9, 1988, October 16, 1988; October 8, 1993; June 23, 1995; April 29, 1996, February 15, 2004 and last amended on January 13, 2008.

Article II

These by-laws shall be binding upon the Shura Committee and all members of Masjid Al Ikhlas, now located at 25 Washington Terrace, Newburgh, New York 12550. The mailing address for the Shura Committee will be: Masjid Al Ikhlas P. O. Box 2117, Newburgh, New York 12550.

Article III

The congregation of members in good standing (attending regular meetings, supporting masjid initiatives, functioning within the guidelines of what is required by our faith and having honorable reputations) shall have the authority to vote on all matters affecting the masjid, masjid holdings, and all of its involvements such as: vote of confidence for the Imam every four years, community direction, property transactions, members of the Shura Committee, etc. Their 2/3's approval indicated by raising the right hand occurring on regular meeting days shall be their vote.

The following components pertain to how one could become an Imam: 1. Election by the Islamic Community (the general masses). 2. Appointment by the outgoing Imam. 3. Approved by a committee (such as the Shura Committee).

According to the Qur'an and Sunnah (i.e. Shariah), the Imam is hereby granted that office for his lifetime with the stipulation that every four years ratification and affirmation (vote of confidence) be taken. This lifetime office does not apply if the Imam deviates from the Noble Qur'an, the authentic Sunnah of Prophet Muhammad (SAWS). If he refuses to accept Shura (mutual consultation) with authenticated dahlil (evidence), the Shura Committee will convene to remove him from The Office of Imam according to the Qur'an and Sunnah regardless of how long he has been in office.

In the absence of the Imam, he will designate one of his assistants to be in charge.

Article IV

The congregation shall appoint the Shura Committee, which will act as a Board of Trustees. Shura Committee members must be declared Muslims and have lifestyles of honorable Muslims established for a minimum of one year at Masjid Al-Ikhlas. The Shura Committee members should be a balanced cross section of the community, whose outlooks transcend race, ethnicity, and culture. Members must uphold the Qur'an and the Sunnah of the Prophet (SAWS). No two family members can serve on the board at the same time.

Tenure: Shura Committee members shall hold office for two or three years, at which time the congregation shall either elect new members or re-elect present Shura Committee members. In any case, Shura Committee members shall be in good health, living sound Muslim lives, and performing well within the capacity of being practicing, good Muslims.

Both Shura Committee members and members of the congregation may nominate someone for the position that has become vacant. The nominee must then be presented at a proper convening of masjid members for approval. As soon as a seat becomes vacant, community members will be made aware at least one week in advance of the next meeting. Position should be filled within one meeting cycle. Nominees must present their resumes to the Shura Committee and then the Imam will present nominees credentials to the community.

Assignment of Duties: The Shura Committee chairperson must assign specific duties to the members of this committee to assure that the aims and objectives of this committee are being met. That is, a specific Shura Committee member may have the duties of assuring payment of utility bills along with and being responsible for the collection of mail or making upkeep and security inspection of masjid and masjid properties. Further, the Shura Committee is to see that masjid and masjid properties are kept well and meet city and fire inspection codes as well as good property and sanitation standards. Shura Committee members must assure that deeds and other important papers are kept in a safe deposit box at a bank. Also, the Shura Committee must act, as fact finders on an as needed basis.

The Shura Committee will be a functionary body insuring the proficient managerial and operational functioning of the masjid and its properties.

Age: The Shura Committee should be capable of handling masjid business in a mature, rational and ethical manner.

Number of Members: The number of Shura Committee members shall be a minimum of seven (7) of which at least two (2) shall be women. In addition, one shall be a youth representative between the ages of 15-18. An alternate's services will be utilized as well. Alternates are expected to be present at each meeting. However, an alternate's services will be utilized only in the event of a regular Shura Committee member's absence. Five (5) Shura Committee members are sufficient for conducting business and establishing policy. Three (3) members need to be present to start a meeting.

As Masjid Al Ikhlas' religious leader and advisor, the Imam may attend Shura Committee meetings; however he is not an official member and, therefore, does not have a vote.

Article V

The Shura Committee is to make monthly reports to the masjid members by way of a bulletin and/or presentations. The purpose of these reports is to keep the congregation informed of current Shura Committee transactions and to bring forth information and concerns surrounding various issues to be addressed by the congregation. Shura Committee reports must be given in the common terms of the English language. The Chairperson of the Shura Committee will keep the Imam abreast of all transactions and activities affecting the masjid.

Article VI

Overriding authority is had first by the Noble Qur'an and then by the authentic Sunnah of the Prophet Muhammad (SAWS). Shura members will also consider the opinions of The Fiqh Council of America, The Islamic Circle of North America (ICNA); The Islamic Society of North America (ISNA) and The Mosque Cares (TMC). Board members and the congregation must also respect the United Sates

Constitution. The congregation must act within the boundaries of the Noble Qur'an and the authentic Sunnah. The Shura members and the congregation will adhere to the sound advice and decisions of the courts of the land as well as all civil and right-minded people without regard to race or national origin.

Article VII

Regular Meetings: The Board, by resolution, may provide the time and place for holding regular meetings without other notice than such resolution.

Special Meetings: Special meetings of the Shura committee may be called by any two members. The persons calling the special meeting may fix the place for holding any special meeting of the Shura called by them. Notice of special meetings shall be given at least twenty-four (24) hours or one (1) day prior to said meeting. Notice shall be in writing and must be given personally, e-mailed, or mailed to each Shura member at his or he home or business address. The notice shall contain the time and place of the meeting along with the topic to be discussed. Preference should be given to holding meetings at the Masjid.

Meeting Attendance: It is expected that all Shura members be present at scheduled meetings. Any board member having three (3) or more unexcused absences will be asked to resign. Unexcused absences have been defined as a person who has not contacted the chairperson by zhur time of meeting day. The chairperson will follow up with members regarding their intentions to remain a part of our Shura committee. A Shura member who is present at a meeting (at which time some action on a matter is taken) shall be presumed to have assented to the action taken unless his or her dissent shall be communicated and entered in the minutes of the meeting.

Article VIII

Power of the Shura Committee to Act: The Shura committee can initiate any action deemed necessary to facilitate the business of the Masjid. The Shura committee shall act as a unit and a majority vote will be the deciding factor in any and all matters pertaining to the Masjid.

Article IX

Amending said By-Laws: Amendment to said by-laws must be approved or ratified by two-thirds (2/3's) majority of Masjid members in attendance on the day that the monthly report is scheduled. Copies of said by-laws are to be made to members of the Masjid congregation at its regular meeting.

APPENDIX B

TIME LINE

This time line was done on Sunday, March 6, 2006 at our Family Day Service
(every First Sunday of the month congregants come to the Masjid
with their families, They bring a meal, juice and dessert).
There were forty –five congregants at this Family Day.

What follows is our time line:

1983

American Muslim Center-six-families met monthly. Imam Warith Deen Umar was the leader then. All the members were apart of Imam Warith Deen Mohammed's community. They met once a month on Sundays.

They purchased a piece of property in Otisville. It was three acres. The name that they chose for this group is "Tie your camel."

There was no Masjid in the Midhudson Valley at this time. Although, There were Muslims meeting in the Poughkeepsie area, and Muslims meeting in the Wappingers Falls area.

1984

The six families continued to meet.

1985

Imam Salahuddin M. Muhammad moves to the Middletown area with his pregnant wife Fonda and son Sharif. He is hired as a NYS Chaplain. Imam Muhammad and wife Fonda join the Islamic community.

1986

Imam Warith Deen Umar takes on a new position in Albany New York, and the community elects Imam Salahuddin M. Muhammad as their leader.

Under the new leadership, the community changes its name to Masjidul Jihadul Akbar. The Muslims met at the New Imam's house for Jumu'ah services on Fridays. Jumu'ah is established. More people are joining the community and we needed to find somewhere else to meet to accommodate the people. The community started meeting in the City of Newburgh at the N.A.A.C.P. building on Liberty Street. The Muslims started having Sunday "Talim" services and weekend school for the children. There were a lot of activities going on with the children. Another member was hired as a NYS Chaplain Malik Shabazz.

1987

Imam Muhammad completes the necessary paperwork to become incorporated and tax-exempt.

January 8, 1987, the Masjid became incorporated, as a non-profit religious organization. The families began to get real tight. New members continue to come/mostly Muslims who migrated to the area. June 25, 1987, received letter of determination for tax-exempt status. We met in the park because we could no longer meet at the N.A.A.C.P. building.

The community had a big event called "I Appreciate My Wife." This banquet brought quite a few Muslims into the area from New York City and the surrounding areas. More Muslims joined us after this event. Imam Muhammad introduced a concept to the community called "Project T.E.A.M." To establish a Masjid as a fund-raising idea. The community was busy trying to raise money for the establishment of a Masjid. Flyers were generated and ads were put in the Muslim Journal newspaper that said "Wanted 100,000 right minded people to contribute $1.00 toward the establishment of a Masjid in Orange County, New York. The dollars started rolling in.

1988

Met in Beacon Community Center across the river/eventually rented a storefront on Main Street in Beacon (167 Main St.). Held Jumu'ah on Fridays/Sundays talim services and weekend school—more believers joining us, as far away as Peekskill and Liberty, New York.

Started United Talim (meeting w/other Islamic communities—Poughkeepsie, Monticello, Beacon—Qasim Muhammad a congregant opens a Halal meat store in Beacon on Main Street near the Masjid.

Events—I Appreciate My Spouse Banquet/Fundraising.

Events—Family Day—each family brings a dish, drinks and dessert the first Sunday of the month. Sometimes we had guest speakers. This continues to be a monthly event.

1989

Interfaith Dialogue, we met with various religious leaders in the community building bridges of understanding. This dialogue happened pre 9/11.

Project T.E.A.M. banquet held, to raise money for the Masjid.

African American/Latinos, Caucasian/Moroccan/Pakistani, Muslims from other Countries started to join us.

An outside person name Dawud Adib came to speak for a weekend, and brought in salafi influence—the community started to change somewhat.—Community begins to split. Some of the ideas caused some of the Muslims to drift away from the ideas of Imam W.D. Mohammed.

1990

Started radio broadcast (Focus on Al Islam WGNY 1220 on the AM dial).

Imam Muhammad, Hafiz Abdur Rahim & Hamin and Melody Rashada go on Hajj to the Holy City of Mecca.

On the international set Iraq invaded Kuwait on 8/2/90.

1991

Communities come together to bring Imam W.D. Mohammed to Poughkeepsie.

Baitul Nasr Established (The House of Help), a non-profit organization started by Muslims to teach, Violent behavior awareness, substance abuse awareness and human development in Poughkeepsie.

Melody Rashada (a woman) becomes treasurer of the Masjid.

The Leadership is questioned/vote taken/1 month new leadership—(Although the Imam won the vote he resigned and the Assistant was the Imam for one month). A new vote was taken and Imam Salahuddin M. Muhammad returned to the position. This was a time of great tension.

On the international set Gulf war, coalition forces begin bombing Iraq. 2/27/91 Kuwait is liberated from Iraq.

1992

Our Masjid experiences its First split—now there are two Masjids in the City of Beacon. The Assistant—Imam left with five families and started their own Mosque.

We purchased a warehouse on nine tenths of an acre in The City of Newburgh (5/19/92)). We used creative financing to avoid paying interest.

Hamin & Melody Rashada found our new home (25 Washington Terrace). We had our first Janazah (funeral ceremony) First Aqeeqah (baby naming ceremony) and first wedding ceremony (Neeqah) on our property.

The first Renovation of warehouse turning it into a place of worship (Masjid).

Muhsinah Shabazz the elder sister in the community began selling fish sandwiches after Jumu'ah to help raise money for the Masjid.

Jenanah Amatullah Muqsit a woman becomes Chair Person of Board of Trustees.

1993

Some members decide to open a Mosque in Peekskill—five to six families leave.

In NYC 2/26/93 first World Trade Center bombing by so-called Muslims.

1994

Egyptians start coming into the Masjid.

Some believers decide to establish a Masjid in Middletown—three or four family's leave.

A Balloon payment $175,000 is due/Mosque only has $35,000. Mortgage renegotiated, several Muslim businessmen come to Mosque's aid—gives us $40,000—we paid $75,000 and paid the rest in monthly installments.

Started father & son breakfast every other week/as well as a yard sale every week, utilizing the property that we owned.

1995

Two Muslims' mothers took shahadah. The assistant Imam (Hamin Rashada's) Mother and the chairperson of the board of trustees (Jenanah A. Muqsit's) mother. This was a very happy moment for the entire community.

Hamin Rashada became a New York State Chaplain.

Some Egyptians broke off and went to the Beacon Masjid, they didn't agree w/our position on woman being in leadership or praying behind the men on the same floor.

1996

Two more New York State Chaplains hired Sisters/Sana Shabazz/Jenanah A. Muqsit.

April 28, 1996 we installed the first Muslim Chaplain at America's finest Military Academy (West Point) Imam Jihad Abdullah.

1997

More Muslims are joining the community. October 11th and 12th we held a big Dawah (propagation) weekend at the Civic Center in Poughkeepsie, New York. This was a collective effort of all the Mosques in the area as well as some from NYC.

1998

Melody Rashada became a New York State Chaplain.

First Tarawih Prayer w/ Hafiz of Qur'an at our Masjid (for the month of Ramadan). Hafiz Muneer, who prayed for the continuous growth of the Masjid.

The balance of what was owed was paid off. The Masjid was free and clear. Allah u Akbar!!!

1999

The community continued to grow. We held another Project T.E.A.M. fund-raising event.

2000

Imam Muhammad and his wife Fonda and Assistant Imam Rashada and his wife Melody go on Hajj to the Holy City of Mecca.

Great influx of many more Muslims from other countries.

Shaikh Reda a graduate of the University of Al Azhar, a Hafiz of Qur'an—Came to work w/us—stayed at Masjid—was paid to teach Qur'an and give classes.

2001

Muslim Community continues to grow. The majority of the Muslims are from other countries now.

April 28th we had an appreciation dinner looking back at fifteen years. We showed appreciation for all those who assisted in maintaining the Masjid.

September 11th second bombing The World Trade center Destroyed. On the international set November 9th War on Afghanistan—Taliban/war on terror.

A lot of Muslim bashing was going on in various cities around the country. The Muslim community in Newburgh received no death threats or harassment, on the contrary the community received a great out pouring of support from the Jewish and Christian Communities—the Jewish women offered to go to the super markets with the Muslim women, if they were afraid to go out. Overall, the Islamic Community did not experience any negative feedback. We believe this was because we had initiated interfaith dialogue back in 1989.

2002

Major Program started Patriot Day (this Program was set up to recognize men and women in our community who go above and beyond the call of duty in terms of giving service. At the first event we recognized two Police Officers in our community—Asadullah Burgos and Sufyana Mahmood.

Imam Muhammad and community participate in Memorial for those lost on 9/11/01 with local religious leaders and their communities.

Shaikh Reda leaves—goes to Florida to become Imam over a community down there. We were not paying him enough to keep him.

Masjid receives major renovations and is also painted inside and outside.

2003

Shaikh Ibrahim comes to us from Morocco by way of Florida. He is a Hafiz of Qur'an and leads the prayers five times a day at the Masjid. After a few months the Shaikh leaves and goes to Connecticut to be an Imam over a Masjid.

Ahmed Rahman (a Pakistani)—becomes the Masjid Treasurer.

Big appreciation BBQ for Imam who had just returned from hip surgery. The Mayor gave Imam a Proclamation for his leadership of seventeen years.

11/12/03—name changed from Masjid Al Jihad Al Akbar, Inc. to Masjid Al Ikhlas, Inc.

2004

Feeling fine at 40—group started by the sisters. The sisters have regular programs for sisters. These classes were religious as well as social gatherings.

A Pakistani family moves to area their son (Uthman Khan) is Hafiz of Qur'an. The Hafiz is seventeen years of age. He starts teaching the children the Qur'an.

Two Muslim doctors purchase property next to Masjid.

2005

8/25/05 Imam participated in unveiling of monument for Rev. Dr. Martin Luther King/also Street named after him in the City of Newburgh.

Groundbreaking ceremony/Mayor, other public officials, and clergy attend and give support to expansion of Masjid.

The two Muslim doctors gift a portion of the property they purchased to the Masjid. The Masjid's property is increased.

2006

Building/Construction—All the framing work is done. The Masjid spends $250,000 for this work and runs out of money. We need to do more fundraising to complete the construction project.

Melody Rashada and Fonda Muhammad started an Activities Committee—To get children more involved in activities like bowling, etc.

The name on the Masjid Deed is changed from Masjid Al Jihad Al Akbar, Inc. to Masjid Al Ikhlas, Inc. The additional property is added to the deed.

Radio Broadcast/put in hands of Sister Kelly Champion /we also changed to a new station (name changed from Focus on Islam to Light on Islam).

2007

In June we have our Grand Re-opening celebration of the completion of the building of the Masjid. In total over $500,000 is spent to complete the Masjid.

2008

In February 2008 we hire Imam Mohammed Ahsan Waris to assist Imam Muhammad in the community. Imam Waris leads all the daily prayers. He is Hafiz of Qur'an and is an Alim. He is our resident Scholar.

We have our first Annual Health Fair and Blood Drive sponsored by our youth.

We start a 90-day pilot weekend school program. This program is a Sunday school program.

Hafiz Uthman Khan starts a brothers meeting as a group on Friday nights.

Because of the success of the 90-day pilot program we officially started our weekend school in September. The name of the Weekend school is "The Islamic Learning Academy of Newburgh."

The radio broadcast is canceled and the community is looking into the possibility of Pod Casting.

Over the twenty plus years I have been the leader of the Masjid, we have had seven treasurers and four Assistant Imams. The treasurers were John Marino, Harold Hasan, Melody Rashada, Asadullah Burgos, Abdul Wahid, Sana Shabazz, and Ahmed Rahman. The Assistant Imams were Harold Hasan, Hamin Rashada, Jihad Abdullah, Asadullah Burgos, and Associate Imam, Mohammed Ahsan Waris.

Appendix C

TRANSPOSING IMAGES PRINCIPLE

figure 8.2 Concealed cow. Drawn by Leo Potishman and published by Da lenbach, 1951.

figure 8.1 Old woman–young woman visual analogy of transposition. awn by cartoonist W. W. Hill, originally published in *Puck*, November 6, 1915. ter published by E. G. Boring, 1950.

Donkey/Seal   Old Man/Young Man   Man/Woman & Baby

figure 8.4 Three reversible images. The donkey/seal image was created by G. H. Fisher (1968). The old-man/young-man image, originally called "husband and father-in-law," was created by Botwinick and published in the *American Journal of Psychology* in 1961. The man/woman/baby image was created by Fisher (1967).

figure 8.3 Can you trust this man? The answer is written all over his face. urther information for answer and reference.)

APPENDIX D

Name_____
Islamic Studies
The Muhammads' Class

QUIZ

Tawheed Class
Article #1: Names of Allah

Read the handout on the "Names of Allah" and review your class notes. On a separate sheet of paper, and in complete sentences, answer the following questions.

1. What kinds of names belong to Allah?

2. What is the Arabic name for "most beautiful names"—a term used to describe all of Allah's names?

3. Silently recite Surah Al-Fatiha, then write down all of the beautiful names of Allah that are mentioned.

4. Name two sources of dalil that mention ninety-nine of Allah's names.

5. Why do Muslims learn the names of Allah?

Fill in the blanks with one of Allah's beautiful names.

6. Allah is the source of **all peace,** and is He is called _____.

7. Nothing resembles Allah; **He is majestic** and is called _____.

8. Allah is **the guardian of our faith,** and He is called _____.

9. Allah is called _____ because He **shows special mercy due to our good works.**

10. **Even if we do not ask for mercy, Allah shows it.** That is why He is called
    _____.

11. When we have losses, **Allah recovers our losses**. He is called _____.

12. Allah is above all evil or bad things. He is called _____ because He is **pure and perfect.**

13. Because Allah **protects in every step of our life,** He is called _____.

14. Allah is **the Mighty and the Strong** and called _____.

15. The one who will **provide for us is Allah**; He is called _____.

16. Allah is **the most loving** and is called _____.

17. Allah **is all knowing** and is called _____.

18. Allah **is all seeing** and is called _____.

19. Allah **is all hearing** and is called _____.

20. Allah **is most forgiving** and is called _____.

List all the ways in which you applied Allah's beautiful names to your life from September 28 through October 12.

1.   6.

2.   7.

3.   8.

4.   9.

5.   10.

BIBLIOGRAPHY

Abdul Rauf, Imam Feisal. *What's right with Islam, A new Vision for Muslims and the West.* HarperCollins Publishers, Inc. NYC, 2005.

Ad-Dimashqi, Al Imam Abu Zakariya bin Sharaf an Nawawi. *Riyadh-Us-Saliheen* vol. 1, Published by Darussalam Publishers & Distributors, Riyadh, 1998.

Ahmad, Shamshad. *Rounded Up Artificial Terrorist and Muslim Entrapment After 9/11.* The Troy Book Makers, Troy, New York, 2009.

Barrett, Paul. *American Islam the Struggle for the Soul of a Religion.* Farrar, Strauss and Giroux, NYC, 2007.

Bolman, Lee G. Terrence E. Deal. *Reframing Organizations.* Published by Jossey-Bass, San Francisco, Ca, 2003.

Denffer, Ahmed Von. *Ulum-Al-Qur'an, an Introduction to the Sciences of the Qur'an.* Published by the Islamic Foundation, United Kingdom, 1983.

Dudley, Carl S. *Studying Congregations, A New Hand Book.* Abingdon Press, Nashville, TN 1998.

Esack, Farid. *Qur'an Liberation & Pluralism, An Islamic perspective of Interreligious Solidarity against Oppression.* Oxford England, 1997.

Ezzati, Dr. Abdul Fazl. Article on the Concept of Leadership in Islam, titled *Tauhid,* from a booklet by the Dawah Academy, International Islamic University, Islamabad, Pakistan in collaboration with the Islamic Teaching Center (ISNA), Plainfield, IN, August, 3-28, 1992 (Second Regional Leadership Training Camp for Dawah Workers).

Fieire, Paul. *Pedagogy of the Oppressed.* Herder and Herder, New York, 1971.

Goldenberg, David M. *The Curse of Ham, Race and Slavery in Early Judaism, Christianity and Islam,* Princeton University Press, New Jersey, 2003.

Graham, Gordon. *A Framework for breaking Barriers—A Cognitive Reality Model.* Gordon Graham & Company, Inc. Bellevue, WA 2002.

Hasan, Ahmad. Principles of Islamic Jurisprudence, the Command of the Shariah and Juridical Norm. Published by Islamic Research Institute, Islamabad, Pakistan, 1993.

Haykal, Muhammad Husayn. *The Life of Muhammad* Translated by Isma'il Ragi A. Al Faruqi. American Trust Publications, Indianapolis, IN 1993.

Jackson, Sherman A. *Islam and the BlackAmerican, Looking Toward the Third Resurrection.* Oxford University Press, N.Y. 2005.

James, William. *The Varieties of Religious Experience.* Harvard University Press, Cambridge, Massachusetts, 1985.

Karim, Dr. Jamillah. *American Women Negotiating Race, Class and Gender within the Ummah.* New York University Press, 2009.

_____. *To Be Black, Female, and Muslim: A Candid Conversation about Race in the American Ummah,* Journal of Muslim Minorities Affairs, Vol. 26, No. 2, August 2006.

Lazear, David. *Eight Ways of Teaching—The Artistry of Teaching with Multiple Intelligences.* Skylight Professional Development. Arlington Heights, IL. 1991.

Leary, Dr. Joy Degruy. *Post Traumatic Slave Syndrome: America's Legacy of Enduring Injury and Healing.* Uptone Press, Milwaukie, Oregon, 2005

Lewis, Bernard. *Race and Slavery in the Middle East, An Historical Enquiry.* Oxford University Press, N.Y. 1990.

Mawdudi, Sayyid Abul A'la. *Towards Understanding the Qur'an.* Published by the Islamic Foundation, United Kingdom, 2006.

Mc Mullin, Rian E. *Taking out your Mental Trash—A Consumer's Guide to Cognitive Restructuring Therapy.* W.W. Norton & Company, Inc. 2005.

_____.The New handbook of Cognitive Therapy Techniques, New York: (W.W. Norton & Company), 2000, 218-232.

Mohammed, Imam Warith Deen. The Mosque Cares, Inc. Collections of Speeches, Writings, Tapes, etc. 1975-2008

Nasr, Seyyed Hossein. *The Heart of Islam, Enduring Values for Humanity.* New York: HarperCollins, 2004.

Phillips, Abu Ameenah Bilal. *The Fundamentals of Tawheed* (Islamic Monotheism). Tawheed Publications, Riyadh, Saudi Arabia, 1990.

Rahman, Fazlur. *Major Themes of the Qur'an.* Bibliotheca Islamica, Minneapolis, MN. 1990.

Schreiter, Robert J. *Constructing Local Theologies.* Published by Orbis Books, Mary Knoll, N.Y. 1985.

Taher, Mohamed, Ed. *Encyclopedic Survey of Islamic Culture, Vol. 1 Islamic Theology,* Anmol Publications. 1997.

Zarobozo, Jamaal Al-Din. *The Authority and Importance of the Sunnah.* Published by Al-Basheer Company for publications and translations, Denver, Co. 2003.

www.studyguide.org/Socratic Seminar.htm

http://qwcine.com/reddick/WorkingWithinCognitiveProgramshtm.

http://quickfacts.census.gov/gfd/states/36/3650034html.

Edwards Brothers Malloy
Thorofare, NJ USA
April 16, 2012